A Children's Book of
Saints

A Children's Book of Saints

by
Hugh Ross Williamson

ILLUSTRATED BY
Sheila Connelly

TREASURE PRESS

Nihil Obstat: ANDREAS MOORE, L.C.L.
Censor deputatis.

Imprimatur: GEORGIUS L. CRAVEN   *Vic. Gen.*
Epus. Sebastopolis.

WESTMONASTERII, *die 24a Aug.* 1960

The Nihil obstat *and* Imprimatur *are a declaration that a book or pamphlet is considered to be free from doctrinal or moral error. It is not implied that those who have granted the* Nihil obstat *and* Imprimatur *agree with the contents, opinions or statements expressed.*

First published in Great Britain as follows:

The Children's Book of British Saints 1953
The Children's Book of French Saints 1954
The Children's Book of Italian Saints 1955
The Children's Book of Spanish Saints 1956
The Children's Book of German Saints 1958

This book, with added material, first published in 1960
by HARRAP LIMITED

This edition published in 1985 by
TREASURE PRESS
59 Grosvenor Street, London W1

ISBN 1 85051 082 2

Printed in Czechoslovakia

50600

CONTENTS

5

PREFACE

THERE are many ways of looking at history and trying to understand how the civilization we live in has been built up and what it means. To Christians, it must always be part of the story of the dealings of God with men, because Jesus Christ came down from Heaven to live and work in the world and to die for it. Since then there have been, in every age, innumerable saints—men and women who, because they loved Christ, cared only for God and His glory and dedicated their lives to it in whatever way was best for their particular gifts in the age and place in which they happened to live.

Here are a few of them. Among them are people of every station in life—kings and queens and statesmen and soldiers and scholars and workmen and housewives and tramps and beggars. The one thing that binds them together is that, before all things, they loved Christ and His Church. The saints are God's messengers in the world, and by looking at them we may be able to understand the real meaning of history.

HUGH ROSS WILLIAMSON

Feast of the English Martyrs, 1960

To
LAURIE EVANS
AND HIS PARENTS

I

ST JAMES THE GREATER

(ST JAMES'S DAY: JULY 25)

IN the year 58 the Apostle Paul told the Romans in his letter to them that he was going to preach in Spain and would call to see them on his way there. We know that when he did get to Rome he was not able to leave that city, but was put to death there by Nero. But, according to tradition, there was already a Christian Church in Spain at least fifteen years before St Paul said he meant to visit it, and that Church was founded by St James the Apostle (who is called 'the Greater' because he was taller than the other St James, who was also a disciple of Jesus).

We can read all that we know for certain about St James the Greater in the New Testament—how he was the brother of St John and shared his nickname as one of the 'sons of thunder,' and how he and Peter and John were the special companions of Jesus at many times, including the occasions of the Transfiguration and the Agony in the Garden of Gethsemane. We know, too, that James was killed by Herod to please the Jews in the year 43 and so was the first of the Apostles to be martyred.

But though we cannot be certain of anything about him except of what is in the Bible, many people in the Church believe that, between the Ascension of Jesus in the year 33 and James's own death eleven years later, he went to Spain and preached the Gospel there; and that his body now lies in the great church of Santiago (St James) de Compostela, which for hundreds of years has been one of the most famous places of pilgrimage in the world.

Certainly James is the Patron Saint of Spain, and the little village, about sixteen miles from Compostela, where a river flows into the sea, is now called simply Padron (which is the Spanish for Patron). It was here that St James is said to have landed and founded the first Christian church in Spain. In those days it was called Iria and was an important Roman town, with a castle known as the 'tower of Augustus'; while Compostela,

It was at Padron that St James is said to have landed

farther inland and standing on a hill overlooking two Roman roads, had the name of Liberodunum.

After St James was martyred in Jerusalem it was said that two of his friends, Phigellus and Hermogenes, put his dead body in a boat and brought it back to Iria, where it was buried, until hundreds of years later the raids of the Norman pirates made the town unsafe and the body was taken to Compostela and reburied there. Our own Anglo-Saxon St Aldhelm, Abbot of Malmesbury, wrote a poem in Latin about it in the year 700 and spoke of St James as the man who "when dear Jesus called him on

10

the seashore, left his home and his own fishing-boat and was the first to convert the Spanish people, turning to God's word the barbarians who worshipped strange gods." And from Aldhelm's day until England gave up the Catholic faith at the Reformation thousands of Englishmen made the pilgrimage to Compostela to the shrine of St James, Patron of Spain.

II

ST DENIS

(st denis's day: october 9)

THERE were Christians in France very soon after the death and resurrection of Jesus. The country, which was then called Gaul, was part of the Roman Empire, so things that were done at Rome soon left their mark there also; and when one of the Emperors, Valerian, ordered a great persecution of the Christians those in Gaul suffered as much as those in Rome. Almost all of them were killed, and after the terror was over the Pope decided he must send some missionaries to preach the Gospel and to encourage those Christians that were left.

The man he chose, who was known to be very brave and good and was very learned in the Christian Faith, was named Denis. Denis took with him his two great friends Rusticus, a priest, and Eleutherius, a deacon; and with some others they travelled the roads of Gaul until they came to an island in the middle of a great river —the island in the river Seine which is now part of Paris. Here they settled and built a church where they began to practise their religion and to preach. They made so many converts that the heathen priests became very angry and asked the Governor Sisinnius to put a stop by force to the new teaching. Sisinnius sent for Denis and his companions, and ordered them to sacrifice to the heathen gods. When they refused to do this they were put in prison and tortured, but they still said that Jesus was truly God and that it was their duty to tell as many people as they could about His resurrection. So they were taken to a high hill overlooking the city and there they were beheaded. That Paris hill is still called Montmartre, which means "the Mount of the Martyrs."

The bodies of Denis and his companions were thrown into the river Seine so that they might float away and be altogether forgotten; but a Christian lady named Catulla rescued them and gave them a proper burial, marking their graves with a little shrine.

Thrown into prison, they refused to worship heathen gods

Years later, when Christianity became the religion of the Roman Empire, a great church was built there so that all Frenchmen might remember Denis, the first Bishop of Paris and "the Apostle of France." Here most of the kings of France were buried. Over the altar the king's standard always hung when he himself was not in battle. And when there were battles to be fought the war-cry of the soldiers was "St Denis for France," for he became the patron saint of France as St George is the patron saint of England.

III

ST HELEN

WHEN the Emperor Constantius died at York in
the year 306 the Roman Army immediately
proclaimed his son Constantine, who was in
Britain with his father, Emperor in his place. The new
Emperor's mother was Helen, who, some people have
said, was the daughter of Old King Cole, the Prince of
Colchester, though others think that she was the daughter
of an innkeeper there. Whichever it was, Colchester is
very proud of her, and there is still a statue of her on the
Town Hall. But the things she did which made her a
saint happened long after she had left Britain with her
son Constantine and gone back to Rome, and in the city
which was named after him Constantinople.

Helen, like most of the people who lived in Britain at
that time, was a pagan, and her son, like her, believed in
the old gods and goddesses of the Romans. But Christianity was getting stronger and stronger, and Constantine had heard about Jesus and the Cross.

Though Constantine had been proclaimed Emperor by
the soldiers at York, there were many powerful people
in other parts of the Empire and in Rome itself who
would not acknowledge him, and he had to fight hard
and for a long time to get the throne. Just before the
battle which would decide everything, he had a dream or
a vision of a flaming Cross in the sky, and the words "By
this conquer." So he made a vow that, if he won the
battle, he would become a Christian, and, more than
that, would make his whole Empire Christian. He kept
his word, and after he had become Emperor made a law

by which Christianity became the religion everywhere the Romans ruled.

Of course, his mother Helen was one of the first to be baptized, and as she learnt about the Cross where Jesus died she began to wonder what had happened to that particular Cross on Mount Calvary. The more she thought about it the more she felt that she ought to go to Jerusalem and try to find it. At last, though she was

They unearthed three crosses

nearly eighty years old, Constantine made arrangements for her to travel to Jerusalem, and told every one there to give her all the help they could. No one thought that she would be able to find the True Cross, for by that time it was nearly three hundred years since Jesus had been crucified. But Helen, in her heart, was quite sure that God meant her to find it.

It had happened that one of the earlier Roman Emperors, Hadrian, who hated the Christians, had built over Calvary and the Holy Sepulchre a terrace three hundred feet long on which was a statue of the Roman god Jupiter and a temple to the goddess Venus. This had been done less than a hundred years after the Crucifixion, so Helen thought that, if she had this terrace destroyed and got down to the foundations, she might find things as they used to be. But even when the workmen had done as she told them, there was an enormous amount of digging to be done, and no real certainty of finding anything.

At last, however, they started to search in a place which Helen had dreamt about, near a little rock-cistern, and there they unearthed three crosses. They all looked very much the same, and there seemed no way to tell which of them was the Cross on which Jesus suffered. But Helen found a very sick man, who was nearly dying, and prayed to God that, if he was laid on the True Cross, he might be cured.

So they took him up and laid him very gently on the first cross. Nothing happened. Then they laid him on the second, and still nothing happened. But when his body touched the third he was immediately cured. So all knew that that was the True Cross, and Helen ordered the builders to build a great church in which it could be kept. A piece of the wood she took back with her reverently to Rome, as well as two of the nails which had been found near it; and when she got home she built there another church called "The Holy Cross in Jerusalem," where the wood and the nails were kept in a shrine.

For hundreds of years pilgrims went from all over Europe to Jerusalem to see the True Cross, until it was destroyed by enemies of Christianity who captured the Holy City; but every year on May 3 the Church still keeps the feast of the Finding of the Cross by St Helen.

IV

ST AMBROSE OF MILAN

(ST AMBROSE'S DAY: DECEMBER 7)

AMBROSE was born in the year 340, not very many years after the Emperor Constantine had made Christianity the religion of the Roman Empire. At that time the Empire had four great governors, and one of these, the Prefect of Gaul (who was responsible for Britain, France, Spain, Portugal, as well as parts of Germany, and for the islands of Sardinia, Corsica, and Sicily), was Ambrose's father. It was natural that Ambrose too should train to become a governor, and he was sent to Rome to prepare himself for his career. When he was twenty-nine he was made Governor of Northern Italy and went to live in the great palace at Milan, where at that time was the Court of the Emperor of the West. He ruled well, and the people came to love and trust him.

Five years after Ambrose became governor the Bishop of Milan died, and there was such a dispute as to who should become the next Bishop that on the day of the election Ambrose decided that he, as Governor, ought to attend in state in case the two different parties began to fight. He spoke to the people, reminding them how they should behave on such a solemn day. Then in the silence after he had finished speaking a child's voice suddenly called out: "Ambrose, Bishop." It seemed like a sign from Heaven. The crowds took up the cry, and the Governor found himself faced by the whole of the city roaring, "Ambrose must be our bishop."

But Ambrose was not a priest. It was quite impossible for him, said Ambrose, to become their bishop. He was their governor, and their governor he would remain. Then, when they still called for him as bishop, he decided to run away. He left secretly at night by a side-door of the palace, and started to travel to Rome. But in the dark he took the wrong turning, and just as day broke he found that he had gone in a circle and had come back to Milan again by another gate. This time the people surrounded him in his palace, and he was practically made a prisoner. So at last he gave in, was baptized, and seven days later made Bishop of Milan. He was thirty-four, and for the remaining twenty-three years of his life he stayed in Milan as Bishop.

He had found when he was governor that it had been difficult to raise enough money to keep the city in proper repair; but with his power then he had been able to tax the people. Now that he had to keep the churches in repair and to find money for the poor he found things still more difficult. He gave away to the Church all his own money and possessions, and made others follow his example. And when people were starving and no more money could be found he decided to sell the gold and silver vessels of the Church itself. His enemies said that this was an insult to God.

"Which do you think is more valuable," said Ambrose, "church vessels or living souls?" And he went on selling the treasures in the market-place, calling, "Behold, the gold of Christ that saves men from death!"

Ambrose's enemies were people called Arians, who claimed to be Christians but who did not really believe that Jesus was God. The Empress herself and most of the courtiers and the wealthy people of Milan were Arians, and at last the Empress, who hated Ambrose, determined to take one of the Christian churches to use for Arian worship. Because she was head of the State she had the right to take any building she wanted, but, all the same, Ambrose knew he must refuse her. He would not allow a

Catholic church to be taken for Arian services. "Palaces are matters for the Emperor," he said, "but churches belong to the Bishop."

The Empress would not listen to his arguments, but ordered her soldiers to occupy one of the churches of Milan. Then Ambrose called on the faithful Christians, and day after day, night after night, they filled every church in the city, saying their prayers, singing hymns, and listening to sermons, so that there was not room for a single soldier to get inside a church. The citizens who had insisted that Ambrose should become Bishop now showed how loyal they were to him. And on Good Friday, 386, the Empress admitted she was beaten and withdrew her order.

Ambrose's next step was to build a great new cathedral (which is known to-day as St Ambrose's) in which he determined to make a shrine for two martyrs, the twin brothers Gervase and Protase, who had given their lives for Christ in Milan over two hundred years before in one of the great persecutions. But no one knew where the martyrs had been buried, and the people did not want to wait until their bones were found—if ever they could be —before the cathedral was dedicated. But Ambrose was sure that the saints themselves would make it possible for him to discover their tomb; and one night the answer was given to him in a dream.

Next day he ordered the workmen to dig in a certain place in front of the railing of a churchyard outside the city gates. The hole was dug, but there was no sign of any bodies buried there. But when it seemed that he had made a mistake an extraordinary thing happened. Blind and lame and sick people who had gone to the place, hoping to find the relics there, were suddenly cured. So the digging began again, and at last the two bodies were found and taken in state to be reburied in the new cathedral. One of the immense multitude who watched this was an African named Augustine, who was later baptized by Ambrose and became one of the greatest of Christian saints.

At the doors of the new cathedral some time later occurred an event which was one of the great landmarks of the early Christian church. In a town far from Milan the Governor had put in prison a charioteer who was a favourite of the people at the games in the Circus. The people thought the sentence was unjust, and they became so angry that they murdered the Governor. When news of it was brought to the Emperor, who was in Milan, he swore that he would take terrible vengeance on the town. Ambrose came to the Emperor, and, while not making light of the crime, asked him to be merciful. Ambrose thought that the Emperor had listened to him, but actually the Emperor sent secret orders to the soldiers of the town that there was to be a great massacre, and seven thousand men, women, and children were murdered.

When the news came to Milan Ambrose called the Emperor a murderer and refused to allow him to receive the sacraments until he had done penance in public. The Emperor said he was sorry, and came to the Cathedral in state, accompanied by his courtiers and his guards. But at the door Ambrose barred the way.

"How can you lift up in prayer the hands that are still dripping with blood?" said Ambrose. "Depart, I say."

"David sinned," said the Emperor; "yet David was forgiven."

"Yes," said Ambrose, "you have imitated David in his sin. Now imitate him in his repentance."

And not until the Emperor put off all his royal clothes and put on sackcloth and in the sight of all Milan confessed his sin, promised amendment, and lay on his face before the High Altar was he allowed once more to receive Holy Communion.

That he was indeed sorry we know, because he enacted

a new law that between the pronouncement of a sentence of death and its execution a whole month must pass, so that there would be time to prevent any injustice. And

At the door Ambrose barred the way

the Emperor so loved and respected Ambrose for showing that the law of God is greater than the law of even the most powerful man that he said, "Ambrose is the only man I think worthy of the name of Bishop."

V

ST GERMAIN

(ST GERMAIN'S DAY: JULY 31)

ABOUT four years after Ambrose was made Archbishop, a boy named Germain was born in Auxerre to one of the noblest families in Gaul, which, like the rest of the Roman Empire, was then, of course, Christian. After studying at the great schools of Arles and Lyons, he went to finish his education in Rome itself. Here he became a lawyer; and so clever and eloquent was he that the Emperor took notice of him and gave him one of the great ladies of the court, Eustachia, as his wife. Then he sent him back to Gaul as one of the six dukes who ruled the country for Rome.

Germain, Duke of Burgundy, went to live in his own town of Auxerre, and held there a magnificent court. Rich and important, he enjoyed himself as much as he could, and, though he was a baptized Christian, did not take his faith very seriously. His favourite sport was hunting, and he used to hang the trophies of the chase on one particular tree which in the old pagan days had been a sacred place.

Amator, the Bishop of Auxerre, went to him again and again, and asked him not to do this because it made some of the simple people who still did not quite understand Christianity think there was not much difference between it and the worship of the old gods. But Germain would not listen to him; and at last one day, when Germain was away in another part of the country, Amator had the tree cut down and burnt all the heads and antlers of beasts which hung on it.

When the Duke came back and found what the Bishop

had done he was so angry that he threatened to kill Amator, and actually set off with some of his soldiers to drag him from the church. But Amator, when they met face to face at the door of the church, persuaded him to come in alone and unarmed. Then Amator did one of the strangest things that any bishop has ever done— though he had got permission from his superiors to do it while Germain was still away. Germain had come to use

He laid hands on him and ordained him as deacon

force on Amator; but once inside the church it was Amator who used force on Germain. The Bishop ordered the doors of the church to be barred against the Duke's attendants and then, against Germain's will, laid hands on him and ordained him deacon.

"Now you must live," he said, "as one who will be Bishop of Auxerre when I am dead."

Germain came out of the church a changed man. He was no longer angry, but accepted what had been done as the will of God. He gave himself up to prayer and good works, he gave away his great wealth to the poor and needy; and when, a very short time afterwards, Amator died he became his successor. The proud Duke of Burgundy had become the humble Bishop of Auxerre.

About ten years later the Church in Britain was in great difficulties. A clever man named Pelagius was preaching something which was not Christian doctrine, but which he pretended was the Faith; and many Christians were following him in his heresy—as this kind of false teaching is called. The Christians who remained faithful sent to the Pope to ask him for some one to help them in arguments against the doctrines of Pelagius. Who was better fitted than Germain, brilliant lawyer and faithful Christian? So Germain, with some companions, crossed to Britain and in a great argument with the heretics at St Alban's showed how wrong Pelagius was.

Germain stayed for some time in Britain, where later he helped the Britons in a very different way—which was a reminder that he had not only been a lawyer but a duke. At this time the Roman garrisons had been withdrawn from Britain, and the fierce Saxon invaders, helped by the Picts from beyond the North Wall, were attacking the British army. Germain suggested to the Britons that as the Saxons and the Picts advanced to give battle they should pray and then give three times the Easter cry: Alleluia! The army did so, and at the sound the enemy fled. Germain's advice had won for the Britons what is known in history as the "Alleluia victory."

When Germain got back to Gaul he found that the people of Brittany had been in rebellion, and he promised to put their case to the Emperor and to ask mercy for them. It was while in Italy on this mission that he died; but, as he had asked, the rebels were forgiven. And, as he asked, too, his body was sent back to be buried at his home, Auxerre.

24

VI

ST PATRICK

(ST PATRICK'S DAY: MARCH 17)

ONE of the companions whom St Germain chose to go with him to Britain was a young man named Patrick who, a few years before, had come to him to study for the priesthood at Auxerre. Patrick had arrived there after many adventures. He was the son of a Roman officer stationed in Britain, and had led the life of an ordinary boy in a wealthy household until, when he was sixteen, he was carried off in a pirate's raid, taken to Ireland and sold as a slave to a chieftain named Milcho. Here his head was shaved, as a sign that he was no longer free; he was given a slave's tunic—a sheepskin reaching down to his knees, and leather sandals—and sent to be a swineherd on the slopes of Mount Slemish. "I was chastened exceedingly and humbled every day," he later wrote about these years, "in hunger and nakedness."

At last he determined to escape. He walked two hundred miles through unknown country until he reached a port where a ship was sailing for Brittany, and persuaded the captain of it to give him a free passage. Once safely in France, he made his way gradually to the region of Auxerre, where some of his mother's relatives lived. He was determined on one thing. Somehow, at some time, he would return to Ireland to bring the faith of Christ to that pagan land ruled in tyranny by the superstitious Druids. But Patrick, though he had great experience of life, had no learning, and he knew that before he could be a priest he had a long training before him.

After his visit to Britain with St Germain, Patrick was

sent to Rome to discuss with the Pope the possibility of a mission to Ireland. The Pope agreed, entrusted it to Patrick, to whom he gave the special title 'Patercuis,' foreseeing that he would be *pater civium*—father of his country—and sent him back to Auxerre to make preparations for the mission.

It was probably in the summer of the year 432 that Patrick, now made a bishop, set sail, and landed not far from Wicklow. He determined that the first thing he must do was to find his old master, Milcho, to pay the price of his ransom, and to convert him, who had been cruel, to the religion of the love of Christ. But as he approached Slemish he saw in the distance a great fire raging in Milcho's fort. The chieftain had heard of his coming and of his power to do miracles and, in a frenzy of rage, had gathered all his possessions together in his house, set it on fire, and thrown himself into the flames, because, says an old record, "his pride could not endure the thought of being vanquished by his former slave."

From one of the chieftains named Dichu, whom he converted on his way to Slemish, Patrick learnt that all the chiefs of Ireland had been summoned by the Supreme King, Laoghaire, to a feast at Tara, where a fire was to be lighted by the Druids as part of the pagan Spring Festival. The day before all other lights had to be put out and not relighted until the 'sacred fire' blazed out on the royal hill. At the opposite end of the valley to the hill of Tara was the Hill of Slane, and it was here that Patrick and his companions arrived on Easter Eve—for the pagan Spring Festival was on the same day as the Christian Easter. (In that particular year Easter Eve was also the feast of the Annunciation.) Patrick went up to the top of the Hill of Slane, and there kindled the Easter fire. When the Druids on Tara saw it they said to King Laoghaire: "This fire which has been lighted in defiance of the royal edict will blaze for ever in this land unless it is put out at once, this very night."

So the King and the Druids and the people all rushed towards the fire, and tried by every means to put it out, and to kill Patrick. But nothing would extinguish the flame, and Patrick, who stood by it singing: "Let God arise and let His enemies be scattered," was preserved from all hurt.

He picked a shamrock-leaf and drew the lesson from its three petals

Next day, at the King's invitation, Patrick went to Tara to tell him of the Christian religion. He knew that there was an ambush to try to kill him on the way, and it was on this occasion, so it is said, that he composed and sang the hymn which is still known as *St Patrick's Breast-plate*, which begins: "I bind upon myself to-day the strong Name of the Trinity," and ends with those words you probably know:

> Christ be with me, Christ within me,
> Christ behind me, Christ before me,
> Christ beside me, Christ to win me,

Christ to comfort and restore me,
Christ beneath me, Christ above me,
Christ in quiet, Christ in danger,
Christ in hearts of all that love me,
Christ in mouth of friend and stranger.

In spite of the ambush, Patrick arrived safely, and after preaching and working signs and wonders before the King, he converted him to the Christian faith, and gained his permission to preach the Gospel throughout the entire land. It was on this day, so men say, that in order to explain to the King the doctrine of the Trinity—how there could be Three Persons in One God—he picked a shamrock-leaf and drew the lesson from its three petals.

St Patrick is rightly called 'the Apostle of Ireland.' To-day we think of him so much in connexion with Ireland that we sometimes forget how much he belongs to Christendom—brought up in Britain by his Roman father, who was a Christian, and receiving his training from the great French saint, Germain.

VII

ST GENEVIÈVE

(ST GENEVIÈVE'S DAY: JANUARY 3)

WHEN St Germain was on his way to Britain he stopped at a little village called Nanterre, about eight miles from Paris. All the people round about came to see the famous man, the Duke who had become a bishop, and when a great crowd had gathered he preached to them. While he was speaking he noticed particularly a little girl who, though she was only seven, was listening very carefully. When he had finished he asked her to come and talk to him. Her name, she told him, was Geneviève; she lived in the village with her parents; and, though she was very young, she had quite made up her mind to spend her life serving Jesus Christ. The Bishop gave her a little medal with a cross engraved on it.

"Wear it always," he said, "to remind you that you have promised your life to Jesus; and be content with it instead of the gold brooches and jewels that you might wear."

When Geneviève was fifteen her parents died and she went to live with her godmother in Paris. Here she led the life of a nun, spending her time in prayer and in doing good to people and, as she grew older, in helping other girls and women who were trying to live the same kind of life.

In her prayers God sometimes allowed Geneviève to see things which were going to happen, but when she warned people about the future they laughed at her and took no notice. Some people even said that she was not really good at all, but was only trying to make a name

29

for herself by pretending to say long prayers and to see visions. Once they got so angry that they even tried to drown her.

Then in the year 451, when Geneviève was about thirty, the people of Paris realized that one of the things she had told them about was really happening. The barbarians were sweeping over Gaul. The last and worst invasion had come. From the east the Huns, led by

Geneviève persuaded the people not to leave Paris

Attila, the "Scourge of God," had reached Gaul, killing, burning, and plundering through all the land. Attila was different from the other barbarian leaders who had begun to attack the countries of the Roman Empire as soon as the Roman army was too weak to defend them. The others had wished to conquer and to rule. The Huns and their leader only wanted to kill and destroy, just for the love of death and destruction; and all men knew they would show no mercy.

The citizens of Paris decided that their only chance of safety was to leave their city and to flee as fast and as far as they could. They were getting ready to do this when Geneviève spoke to them. She told them that they were wrong, and that if they really trusted in God and prayed to Him, if they really repented of their sins and showed they were in earnest by doing penance for them, they would be spared. Some of the people were still in favour of flight, but others remembered that in the past Geneviève had told them the truth even if they had not believed her—and gradually the city became calm again. The citizens would do as she said—and wait.

And then, by what seemed a miracle, Attila changed his course. Instead of taking the road to Paris, he suddenly altered his direction and turned off towards Orléans, leaving the capital untouched.

VIII

ST BRIGID

ABOUT the same time as St Geneviève was living in France there was in Ireland another great woman who was to become a saint. Her name was Brigid (or Bridget, as it is sometimes wrongly called). Her father was a chieftain and her mother a slave in his household with whom he had fallen in love. Many wonderful stories are told of Brigid's childhood—how wild birds would become tame and let her stroke them, and how the linnet would sing its first song for her. Men said of her: "She dips her fingers in the stream and the ice melts. She breathes upon the world and the winter is gone." There was a tale that when she worked in the dairy she would only half fill a jar with butter, saying: "God will add something to it," and each jar would become miraculously full. And when she was looking after sheep in the fields she would pray by a flat white stone which she called her altar, and which, to make it balance evenly, had been given four small feet by an angel.

What was certain about Brigid was that from a very early age she loved God and wished to serve Him as a nun. Because of her beauty, many young noblemen wished to marry her, but she refused them all, and at last left her father's house, with some friends, to offer herself to do God's service in whatever way her bishop thought best. The bishop said, "You shall be called Sisters of Mercy," gave them white robes of nuns, and made them promise to give up their lives to serving God by prayer and works of charity.

Brigid and her companions chose as their first home

32

a house under a great oak-tree, which they called Cill Dara—"the Church of Oak"—and which later grew into the city of Kildare. Her convent soon became the centre of religion and learning. She founded, too, a school of art, where metalwork and illumination of manuscripts was taught. The finest work produced there was an illuminated book of the Gospels, which disappeared at the Reformation but which those who saw it said had no equal. Every page was most gorgeously

Many wonderful stories are told of Brigid's childhood

painted, with such elaborate designs, that according to an old chronicler the colours seemed "the work of angels, not human hands," and the story arose that night after night, as Brigid prayed, "an angel furnished the designs which the scribe copied."

The fame of Brigid spread far and wide. Her city of Kildare, with its Cathedral and its school, became famous all over Europe. She was known as Patroness of Ireland and "Queen of the South": and when she died the great shrine over her tomb was visited by pilgrims from all over Christendom.

33

IX

ST BENEDICT

(ST BENEDICT'S DAY: MARCH 21)

BENEDICT was born about the year 480 in the Castle of Norcia, in the hilly country of Central Italy. His father sent him to study in Rome when he was about fourteen, hoping that he would become a lawyer. But Benedict did not like the life he saw in the capital. In those days men never knew what new horde of barbarians might suddenly raid Italy. Nothing was settled, and people, thinking that any day they might find their homes and their ways of life destroyed, lived just to enjoy themselves. Like the foolish man that Jesus told about in one of His parables, they said, "Let us eat, drink, and be merry, for to-morrow we die."

Even when he was a boy of fifteen Benedict was sure that this was the wrong way to live; so one day, with the old family nurse, Cyrilla, who was looking after him in Rome, he ran away to live in a cave among the mountains. He thought that by being alone, far away from the wild ways of the city, he would be able to see things more clearly and find out how God wanted him to live. And it was not long before he decided he must leave even his nurse and be quite alone by himself. One night he ran away from her, and travelled till he came to a barren, rocky place among the mountains called Subiaco, where some other hermits lived. Here he found a cave underneath the ledge of a great rock rising out of a lake. One of the other hermits used to bring him regularly some bread, which he lowered by a rope into Benedict's cave; and here he lived for three years.

During this time people in the surrounding countryside started to talk about this young nobleman who had gone into the desert to listen to God. Some shepherds, wandering through the valley, saw him come out of his cave to gather herbs. He wore a rough dress of animal skins, and from the distance they thought he was an animal himself until he stood up. Then they went up to him and knelt and asked him to bless them. Later some people in a little village not far away heard of him and brought the sick to him, asking him to heal them. And one Easter morning a monk from a monastery in the district took some food and drink to Benedict's cave and insisted on talking to him.

"Come, let us eat together," he said, "for it is Easter."

"Indeed it is Easter," answered Benedict, meaning that it was a day of great joy to him to be visited by some one else who was trying to do God's will.

"It is *really* Easter Day," said the monk, who realized that Benedict had been alone too long to know what day —or even what month—it was. "No one should fast on Easter Day, and I have been sent to give you these gifts by Almighty God. As I was sitting down to eat I heard God saying to me, 'You are preparing to feast, while my servant Benedict is starving to death on the other side of the valley.' So I have brought my meal to share it with you."

Benedict was very grateful, because by this time he really was almost starving. The hermit who had brought him the bread which he let down on a rope did so no longer, because he thought that Benedict was dead.

When the abbot of the monastery from which the monk had come died the monks asked Benedict to come and be their abbot. At first he refused, because he knew that they were living there not so much to listen to the voice of God as to have a comfortable time far away from the dangers of the world. He had come alone into the desert because he wanted to find some new way to live

35

in the troubled and evil times; they had come away because they wanted to go on living very much as they had before, without the risk of the barbarians destroying them. But at last he gave in and became their abbot. He was so strict that one of the monks tried to poison him; and the story says that when he made the sign of the Cross over the cup at the beginning of the meal it suddenly smashed, and the poisoned wine was spilt over the table. (That is why in pictures of St Benedict you will usually find him holding a cup.) Benedict said, "May God have mercy on you, my brethren. Why have you done this to me? Did I not tell you before that there was nothing in common between my manner of life and yours? Go and find the kind of abbot you want, for you can no longer have me." And he went back to his lonely cave.

But by this time so many people had heard of him and had come out to Subiaco to live in cells near him that he was forced to make some arrangement for looking after them; and before many years were over twelve monasteries had been founded there, all looking to Benedict as their 'Father,' and living by the new rule he drew up for them. This rule, which is still known as the Benedictine Rule, and which thousands of monks still keep, was a plan for life in a monastery—so many hours to be given to prayer, so many to work, and so many to sleep. It was the answer God had given to Benedict, who had run away from the life of Rome and asked how men could best live in those troubled, terrible times.

Benedict did not stay all his life at Subiaco. After he had founded his monasteries and given them his Rule he went away again to be by himself at the top of another lonely mountain called Monte Cassino. But once again men followed him, wanting to be near so good and great a man of God, and at Monte Cassino there grew up the most famous monastery of all, which like the others was 'a school of service to God.' It is still there—much larger than it was in Benedict's day—and although in the great war of 1939–1945 it was damaged in battle, men of all nations helped to repair it again.

At the foot of the mountain Benedict's twin sister, Scholastica, founded a nunnery, where women could come and live under the same Benedictine Rule. And

Scholastica could not bear to let Benedict go

once every year—because that is all that the Rule allowed —the brother and sister would meet at a hut on the mountain-side, half-way between them. At one of these meetings when they were both getting old Scholastica could not bear to let Benedict go. She asked him to stay a little longer, but he said that he and she must obey the Rule just like every one else and that the Rule did not allow them to stay. Scholastica bowed her head on her hands and prayed. It was a lovely evening, with not a cloud in the sky. Then suddenly there was a peal of thunder, flashes of lightning, and a torrent of rain so heavy that no one could go out in it.

"May God pardon you, sister," said Benedict; "what have you done?"

"I asked you to let us stay together a little longer," said Scholastica, "and you would not listen to me. So I asked God, and He has listened."

Three days later Benedict had a dream in which he saw his sister flying up to Heaven in the form of a dove, and soon afterwards news was brought to him that she had died at the very moment that he had seen it in the dream. He had her body brought up to Monte Cassino and buried in the grave that he had prepared for himself, and it was only a few weeks later that he fell ill of a fever and was laid with her in the same tomb.

X

ST GREGORY THE GREAT

(ST GREGORY'S DAY: MARCH 12)

GREGORY was born in Rome ten years before St Benedict died. He was the son of rich parents who lived in a great palace on the Cælian Hill, and while he was still a young man he was made Prefect of Rome. This meant that he was the most important man in the city, rather like the Lord Mayor of London. He wore a purple cloak and rode in a magnificent chariot drawn by four snow-white horses. Then suddenly he gave it all up, and the Romans saw him "who used to go about the city clad in the purple and aglow with silk and jewels, now in a worthless garment serve the altar of the Lord." Gregory had met some of St Benedict's disciples, and had determined himself to become a Benedictine monk.

He sold all his estates in Sicily, and with the money he got for them he founded six monasteries. His great palace on the Cælian Hill he turned into another monastery, which he dedicated to St Andrew, and of which he later became the abbot.

It was during the first years which he spent there as a monk that one day he was walking in the city when he saw some fair-haired young slaves for sale.

"Who are they, and where do they come from?" he asked.

"They are Angles, and they come from Deira," he was told.

"Not Angles, but angels," said Gregory, "and they shall be saved from the wrath of God." (*De ira* is the Latin for 'from wrath.') Then he asked the slave-owner, "Who is their king?"

"Aella is his name," answered the man.

"Then Alleluia must be sung in Aella's land."

He determined that he would make the journey to far-off England and preach the Gospel to the pagan Saxons and Angles there. But just at that time it looked as though some new barbarians were about to break through and threaten Rome itself, and the Pope decided to send word to the Emperor at Constantinople of what

"Not Angles but angels," said Gregory

was happening and ask his help to guard the west. Gregory's long training and his work as Prefect of Rome made him the most suitable man to send, and so he found himself not converting the islanders in the north but acting as an ambassador in the east.

Even when his work there was done and he came back to his beloved monastery of St Andrew he was not allowed to please himself, and before long he was elected Pope. Just as Ambrose, two hundred years before, had run away when people called for him as Bishop of Milan, so now Gregory—who was in many ways very like

Ambrose—ran away from being made Bishop of Rome. But, like Ambrose, he was brought back, and he ruled the city till his death. And one of the first things he did when he became Pope was to send a party of his monks, headed by one called Augustine, to England to bring Christianity to the land of the fair-haired slave-boys.

In the same year, 597, that Augustine landed in Kent, St Columba, an Irishman who had taken the Gospel to Scotland, died.

XI

ST COLUMBA

THE little Irish prince was christened Colum, which means 'a dove.' As he grew up he became very strong and tall, and every one who saw him said he looked like an angel. He took no part in the fierce fighting of the clans, but when he was quite young decided to be a priest and to build monasteries, where men could live together in peace, praising God, teaching the people, and going out into the country around telling the heathen about Jesus Christ.

Many of these monasteries he founded in Ireland, and then one day a sad thing happened. There was a quarrel between the tribes which led to fighting and bloodshed, and in some way Columba—the 'dove'—had had something to do with it. We do not know exactly what it was, but, as a prince who was fond of his own people, he may have taken sides and forgotten for a moment his duty as a priest. Whatever it was, he was terribly sorry for it, and to show how great was his sorrow he determined to do for the love of God the most difficult thing he could think of. He would leave the land and the friends he loved so much and go over the sea to Scotland, where, away in the north, were the wild Picts who had never heard of Christ.

So one day, with twelve friends who were monks like himself, he set sail in a boat made of wickerwork covered with the skins of animals—a coracle—called *The Dewy Red*. They took with them a few provisions to last them till they got to the other side, but, although they were going among fierce men, they took no weapons. They

42

were dressed in long robes of white wool, with nothing but sandals on their feet.

At last they reached one of the islands just off the coast of Scotland and landed on it. Columba looked back over the sea, and there, far, far away, he could just see the shores of Ireland.

"We cannot stay here," said Columba. "We must get in our boat again and go farther on."

There they decided to stay

"Why must we do that?" asked his companions. "This seems a good island to build our monastery on."

"It is a good island," said Columba, "but we must go on farther because from here we can still see our home. If day by day we look at it over the sea our hearts will always be going back there. Let us go where we cannot see it, and then we shall be more content to live among strangers in a strange land."

So they got in their coracle again and went farther on, till they came to another island which was called Hy, but which is now called Iona. They scrambled on to the shore and looked back over the sea. But this time they could see nothing but the waves. The shores of Ireland had disappeared in the distance.

"This is our island, surely?" said the monks.

"We must make quite sure," said Columba. "Let us climb to the very highest part of the island, for we might be able to see home from there."

But even from the top of the highest hill they could see nothing, so there they decided to stay. On the hill they made a little pile of stones, called a cairn, and they named it Carn-cul-ri-Erin, which means the Cairn of the Back-turned-to-Ireland. And on Iona they stayed, and built their first monastery.

It was their outpost in a new land, and from it these soldiers of Christ made their expeditions into the wild pagan country around. The King of the Picts, Brude, lived far away at Inverness, surrounded by dark forests where wild animals still roamed, and by unknown mountains and glens and lochs. There was no road, and even the Roman soldiers had not been able to push their way through. But Columba and his white-robed monks managed to get there.

They took, of course, a long time on their journey, and by the time they got to Brude's palace the King had heard from his people that they were coming, and had barred the gates against them. Fierce Pictish warriors guarded the gates, ready to fight the newcomers if they were attacked. But the monks carried no weapons; only their staves to help them in the journey—and a wooden Cross.

Columba walked straight up to the bolted and barred gates and, raising his hand, made the sign of the Cross upon it. Immediately, of its own accord, it opened and swung wide. The guards ran away in terror to tell the King what had happened. They thought that Columba must be some powerful magician. But King Brude was not frightened. He left the heathen priests who were with him and came and welcomed Columba, and asked him to tell him who he was, and why he had come to see him. So Columba told him about Jesus Christ, and how he had journeyed so far to bring him the Good News of the Gospel. The two became great friends.

When Columba got back to Iona he found that there were many other places to which he could send missionaries. His monks went out all over Scotland, and even into England, preaching; and more and more people came to Iona to help him.

In those days all books had to be written by hand, and Columba himself made copies of the Gospels and the Psalms to send out by his missionaries. One night as he was working in this way he grew very tired, and he knew that he had not long to live. He was seventy-six years old, and his life had not been easy. When he got to the verse, "They who seek the Lord shall want no manner of thing that is good," he said to those round him, "Here I must stop. Others must write what follows." It was a Saturday morning when he told them, "This is the last day of my life of labour on earth; at midnight, when the solemn Day of the Lord begins, I shall go the way of my fathers."

Through that night he sat up in his cell, where he had a bare rock for a mattress and a stone for a pillow, and as the bell rang for Matins he went into the church. Dermot, one of the monks, followed quickly and called, "Where are you, Father?" It was quite dark, for the lamps had not yet been brought in, and he could not see Columba. Nor was there any answer. Groping his way, he found Columba lying on the altar steps, unable to speak.

Meanwhile the other monks had come in with lights, and when they were all there Columba managed to move his hand a little, and they knew that he was giving them his last blessing. Then he died, but his face was so happy and peaceful that he seemed to be living and sleeping. They buried him in Iona, but years later, when the Danes started their invasions, burning churches and monasteries, the body of Columba was taken for safety across the sea back to the Ireland he had loved and left.

XII

ST HERMENGILD

(ST HERMENGILD'S DAY: APRIL 13)

WHEN the barbarian tribes overran and conquered the Roman Empire those who took Spain and ruled there were called Visigoths. Though the Visigoths became Christian, they soon fell into the 'Arian' heresy which was very powerful all over Europe. The Arians, though they called themselves Christians, did not really believe that Jesus was God, and you may remember how hard St Ambrose had to fight against them in Italy.

Leovigild, King of the Visigoths, who ruled in Spain from 569 to 586, had two sons: Hermengild and Reccared. Both the boys were brought up as Arians, but when Hermengild was old enough to marry his father chose for him a Frankish princess as bride and sent him to govern that part of Spain of which the capital was Seville. Hermengild's wife was a Catholic, and there was in Seville at that time a great Catholic bishop, St Leander. Before long Hermengild had listened to their teaching and given up his Arianism and became a Catholic too.

King Leovigild was very angry when he heard this. His wife had died and he had married again, this time a woman who was an even stricter Arian than he himself. And she gradually brought him to hate Hermengild so much for his becoming a Catholic, that he ordered his son to leave Seville unless he would give up his religion. Hermengild, of course, refused, and his father marched against Seville with a great army.

Hermengild held out for two years and then managed

to escape to Cordova where he took refuge in a church and, when the King and his army followed him, refused to leave the altar. Leovigild then sent his other son, Reccared, to promise Hermengild a free pardon if he would come out and submit to him. Hermengild believed his brother, but as soon as they returned to their father, Leovigild, after giving him the kiss of pardon,

Ordered him to be sent into banishment

ordered him to be stripped of his royal clothes, loaded with chains, and sent into banishment at Valencia.

Here Hermengild was kept in prison while his stepmother urged his father to have him put to death unless he would give up the Catholic faith and become an Arian again. At Easter, in the year 585, Leovigild sent an Arian bishop to Hermengild's prison to celebrate Mass with him and to tell the Prince that if he would partake of it everything should be forgiven. But Hermengild, as soon as he found that the Bishop was not a Catholic, refused.

"You call yourself a Christian," said the Bishop, "yet you refuse to receive Holy Communion."

"What you could offer me," said the Prince, "is not the Body and Blood of Jesus, for you are no true Bishop."

"You will not even love and obey your father?" said the Bishop.

"I love him," said Hermengild, "but I cannot obey him, because I love God more."

When this was reported to the King, he became so violently angry that at last he did as his Arian wife asked, and ordered soldiers to go to Hermengild's prison and kill him. With an axe they split open his head. And so died a Prince who preferred to give up his life and his throne rather than deny his belief in Jesus by receiving Holy Communion at the hands of a heretic.

XIII

ST ISIDORE OF SEVILLE

(ST ISIDORE'S DAY: APRIL 4)

ST LEANDER of Seville—who, you remember, was the friend and supporter of Hermengild—had a young brother named Isidore. Isidore was born at Cartagena, where his father was the Roman Governor, but he was sent to school at Seville, where his elder brother became one of his teachers. The school at Seville was the first of its kind in Spain. All the ordinary school subjects were taught, and the boys were made to work very hard. Isidore, like many boys, disliked hard work, and one day he played truant from school. In fact, he intended to run away altogether; but, as the sun was very hot and he soon became very tired, he sat down to rest beside a little spring that gushed over a rock. As he was resting in the shade he noticed that the stone on which the drops of water fell had been worn away, and he thought: If drops of water can actually make a hole in a hard stone by never ceasing to fall, surely if I persevere with my lessons I shall gradually get to like them and not find them so dull and difficult. So that evening he went back to school and before long became the best scholar there.

When he grew older he became a teacher in the school, and when his brother, St Leander, died he was made Bishop of Seville in his place. The King at that time was St Hermengild's brother, Reccared, who had persuaded Hermengild to come out from the safety of the church and had helped his father to deceive him. But when Reccared had become King he had also become a Catholic, for he never forgot the example of Hermengild's bravery and he could not help feeling that he was partly to blame for his death. So, with the King a Catholic and the two great Bishops, St Leander and St Isidore, to teach the people, it was not long before Arianism was destroyed in Spain.

But Isidore saw that he had other work to do. The long rule of the barbarian Goths in Spain had meant that the country had become uncivilized. Men had forgotten

He set to work to compile the first encyclopædia that had been made in Christian times

all the learning which the Roman Empire had given them. They had even forgotten to have any manners. Isidore thought that if Spain was to become a great land again, worthy of the Catholic faith, the young people must be educated once more. First of all he made the school at Seville even better than it had been in his brother's time. Greek and Hebrew and law and medicine could all be studied there. And he himself set to work to compile the first encyclopædia that had been made in Christian times, so that those who wanted would have a great reference book of all branches of knowledge.

Then, in the year 633, when he presided over a Church Council at Toledo, where all the bishops in Spain met together, he persuaded them that schools like his at Seville should be attached to every cathedral in the country. When Isidore died three years later, one of these bishops, Braulio of Saragossa, wrote of him: "I think that God must have raised him up in these times to restore Spain from the decay into which it has fallen, to set up again the ancient landmarks, and to save us from becoming altogether barbarian."

For hundreds of years men all over Europe (including our own Venerable Bede) owed a great debt to St Isidore, who understood that sound learning is part of the Christian life, and who was nicknamed 'the schoolmaster of the Middle Ages' because men continued to use for many years the books he wrote.

XIV

ST AIDAN

(ST AIDAN'S DAY: AUGUST 31)

ONE of the monks in the monastery of Iona was named Aidan. He was one of the kindest and simplest of all the monks there. One day the Abbot called him and told him that he was to go away from Iona to the court of Oswald, King of Northumbria, to preach the Gospel to the Northumbrians.

Oswald was a Christian who had been driven from the the kingdom by the heathens, and while he was hiding from his enemies in Scotland he had visited Iona. Now that he was King, after defeating the heathen in a great battle, he wanted to make the whole kingdom Christian, and, naturally, it was to his friends at Iona that he sent to ask for teachers and missionaries. The first of the monks to go was named Corman, but he was not able to do very much. He soon came back and told the others at Iona, "You cannot teach the English. They are barbarians. They have no manners, and they will not try to learn."

"Perhaps," said Aidan, "you have been trying to teach them things that are too difficult. When you feed a baby you give it milk, not meat. These men are like babes in learning, and you must treat them like that."

When the Abbot heard this he was sure that Aidan was the best man to send, because he was so simple and kind; and so he was chosen to go into Northumbria.

Aidan soon became a great friend of King Oswald, who was himself a saint, and both of them tried to live in such a way that every one could see that they were followers of Jesus. They were especially kind to the poor, and one Easter Day when they were having a meal together in the King's palace they heard that a great crowd of beggars had gathered outside hoping for some scraps left over from the royal feast. Immediately they stopped eating the splendid food that had been set before them, and the King gave orders that the whole meal was to be given to the beggars. Not only the food was to go to them, but the silver dishes on which it was served were to be broken up and distributed among the poor.

Oswald gave Aidan a small island called Lindisfarne, just off the coast of Northumberland, so that he could build a monastery on it like the one at Iona. Lindisfarne soon became known as Holy Island. The buildings were not much more than wooden sheds, and the monks lived on milk and bread and vegetables; but from here they went out into the countryside around preaching and founding churches.

Aidan himself used to walk, whether he was in the towns or in the country, and never go by horseback unless there was some important journey he had to take quickly. He spoke to every one he met, whoever they were. If they were heathen he told them about Jesus Christ, and urged them to believe and be baptized. If they were Christians he asked them if they were living good lives and doing all they could for Christ, so that the heathen would see their example.

It seemed as if the whole of Northumbria would soon become Christian because of the work of Aidan and the monks of Lindisfarne, and of the help given them by King Oswald. But just on the borders of his kingdom Penda, the pagan King of Mercia (the part of England we now call the Midlands), was preparing for war. Penda hated the Christians, and he hated Oswald for being a Christian. Already Penda had killed four Christian kings, and now he was ready to go to war again to try to kill Oswald and take his land and burn down all the churches that Aidan had founded. Oswald got his army together and marched to meet Penda, but in the great battle that followed the Northumbrians were defeated and Oswald himself was killed.

Then Penda marched up through Northumbria, burning and destroying the churches and killing the Christians. On he went, with no one to stop him, till he came to the walls of Bamburgh, which had been Oswald's capital.

He spoke to every one he met, whoever they were

But Bamburgh, with its castle, was so strong and well defended that he was not able to take it. So he decided to burn it. He sent his soldiers into all the villages round about with instructions to destroy them, but to bring to him everything that would burn. The soldiers collected a great heap of planks and beams and wattle and rubbish and brought it to the walls of the town. It looked like an enormous bonfire—and that was exactly what Penda meant it to be. As soon as the wind blew in the direction of Bamburgh he set light to it, and waited for the

55

flames to spread into the castle and the town and destroy them.

On Lindisfarne Aidan saw the flames. He understood what was happening. The fire and the smoke were being carried by the boisterous wind over the walls, and in a few moments Bamburgh would be no more. Aidan fell on his knees and, raising his eyes and his hands to Heaven, he said, "You see, Lord, what a great mischief Penda is doing!" And at that moment the wind suddenly changed, turned from the town, and drove back the flames on Penda and his army. Bamburgh was saved, for after that Penda returned to his own country, and Oswald's brother became King of Northumbria and allowed Aidan to continue his preaching.

It was while he was staying in the royal palace near Bamburgh that Aidan died. He was suddenly taken ill while he was on one of his visits to the countryside round about, and the King's servants, with the monks who were with him, put up a tent for him outside the west door of the church there, so that he might be near the altar. At his last moment, like his master, St Columba, he tried to make his way to the altar, but he was too weak, and he died resting on a buttress which had been placed against the outer wall for the support of the church. But the monks took his body back to Lindisfarne, the Holy Island, and buried it there.

XV

ST AUDRY

(ST AUDRY'S DAY: OCTOBER 17)

AUDRY, whose other name was Etheldreda, was a princess. She was born in the little Suffolk village of Ixning, and when she was very young her parents gave her in marriage to one of the princes of East Anglia. He died very soon after they were married, and Audry went to live in that part of the country which had been given to her as her dowry, the Isle of Ely. It was called an island because at that time it was surrounded by waters and marshes, and it got its name from the great number of eels which could be caught there.

Her plan was to build on this land a nunnery where women could live together and serve God as the monks did, and she had made up her mind exactly where she would start building when her uncle, who was now king, told her she was to marry again. In those days kings increased their land and power by letting their sons and daughters marry into the families of other kings, and the man chosen for Audry to marry was the prince of Northumbria, the nephew of King Oswald, who would one day himself be King.

Audry told her uncle that she did not wish to make this marriage, but that all she wanted to do was to give her life to God; to become a nun, and to build a nunnery on her own land.

"But if you make this marriage," said her uncle, "one day you will be a great queen."

"I do not want to be a queen," said Audry. "I want to be a nun."

"There are many ways of serving God," answered her

57

uncle. "You can serve Him just as well at Court as in a nunnery. And besides, by marrying a powerful prince you will be doing great good to the people here."

After a time Audry decided that she ought to do as her uncle asked, and she was married to Prince Egfrid of Northumbria with great pomp and splendour. But she told the Prince that, although she would do faithfully all the duties that would fall on her, she could never be a loving wife to him, because her heart was in Ely, where, for the love of God, she wanted to build her nunnery. When Egfrid became king he thought that in time she would forget this and settle down with him as Queen. But he was wrong. Life at Court only made her want more and more to go back to her home, and, though she was fond of Egfrid, she was quite sure she was never meant to be his wife. With tears she asked him again and again to let her go back. Again and again he refused.

At last one day he said yes. She could hardly believe her ears, and she set off at once, before he would have time to change his mind. The journey back to Ely was long, so, as the first stage of it, she decided to go to the nunnery at Coldingham, where her aunt, Ebba, was the abbess. She would become a nun at once, so that if Egfrid did change his mind and want her back it would be impossible for her to go.

As a matter of fact, no sooner had she left the palace than Egfrid was sorry that he had ever said she might go, and called a band of soldiers and told them to follow her and bring her back. But they missed the way, and Audry arrived safely at Coldingham, where she immediately took the veil of a nun.

"Egfrid is a good man," she said. "Now that I have taken this vow to serve God, he will leave me in peace."

But Ebba said that it might be wiser not to stay at Coldingham but to get outside the boundaries of Northumbria. She was right. As soon as the soldiers got back to Court to tell Egfrid that they had not been able to find Audry before she took refuge in Coldingham he determined to set off to the nunnery himself, with an army, to bring her back by force. Audry had already left Coldingham by the time he arrived, but one of the people in the district pointed out the way she had gone, and Egfrid set off quickly in pursuit.

He came up with her at a place called Coldeburgh

The sea suddenly swirled round the rock

Head, a great rock jutting out to sea. She was in disguise, and had with her the two serving-women who had left Court with her. Egfrid was just about to scramble on to the rocky headland to seize her when the sea suddenly swirled round the rock and cut it off from the mainland. The King and his men found they could not cross, so they waited until the tide should go down and the crossing should be possible. But the tide did not go down. Day after day went by, and still the sea protected Audry and her attendants. Egfrid at last decided that this was

59

a sign from Heaven that God wished Audry to live the life she had chosen, so he said good-bye to her and rode away, leaving her to continue her journey to Ely.

When the sea had subsided Audry and her two companions left Coldeburgh Head, and, as they were still not quite sure that Egfrid would not follow, they went by byways and lanes, dressed as pilgrims, begging their bread. At last they arrived safely at Ely, and a great welcome was given to Audry by her own people, and especially by her brother, who was now the King. As soon as she was rested from her journey she began to make plans for building the church and the abbey where the nuns she hoped would come to live with her could serve God in their special way.

That was the beginning of the great Cathedral of Ely, and for hundreds of years there was a fair held near it called "St Audry's Fair." Here they sold brightly coloured laces and ribbons, perhaps to remind people of the splendour which St Audry gave up when she refused to be a queen. Poor people would sometimes put these ribbons as little offerings on her tomb, and they became known as "St Audry's laces," or 'tawdries.'

XVI

ST CUTHBERT

(ST CUTHBERT'S DAY: MARCH 20)

IN the valley of the Tweed, the river which divides England from Scotland, there lived a shepherd-boy named Cuthbert. He was very strong and lively, spending all the time he could in games and sports, and being so good at them that he usually beat his companions in jumping and running and wrestling. Then one day something went wrong with his knee. It started to swell, and though the doctor tried to heal it, it got worse and worse. Cuthbert could no longer run about. He found it difficult even to walk. He thought he would be a cripple all his life.

But, as it turned out, he was lucky. A traveller who was passing through the valley saw him and told him of a way in which his knee might be cured. Cuthbert tried it, and he was soon quite well again—so well that he went for a short time to be a soldier in the King of Northumbria's army. But he did not ever forget the time when, because he could not lead an ordinary life like the others, he was so lonely, and was asking God to make his knee better. In the end he was to become a hermit—that is, a man who lives all alone so that he can have more time to say prayers for other people.

This did not happen for many years, though soon after he came home from the war he made up his mind to become a monk. One night, when he was looking after his sheep on the Grampian Hills, he suddenly saw a great light in the sky. Wondering what it could be, he looked more closely, and saw a band of angels coming down to earth and then going back into the skies carrying some one in their arms.

As the light faded he went over to his companions and asked them one by one what they thought it was. But none of them had seen it. Some of them had been asleep, and those who were awake had seen no light, and told Cuthbert that he must have been asleep and have dreamt it all. It was not till many days afterwards that Cuthbert heard the news that on that night, far away in Northumbria, St Aidan had died; and then he knew that, whether it was a dream or whether it was a vision, it was God's way of telling him that He wanted him to come and serve Him in the same kind of way as St Aidan had chosen.

So as soon as he could arrange for other people to look after the sheep for their owners he set out for the nearest monastery, which was at Melrose, and there he became a monk. Later on he was sent to Lindisfarne itself, and for twelve years was Prior there. Yet all the time he really wanted to be a hermit, and at last the Bishop let him have his wish.

Not far from Lindisfarne was a tiny island—an islet—named Farne. No one lived on it, because people said that it was full of evil spirits; and there was no water there, or trees; and corn would not grow. But Cuthbert determined to make his home there, and the brethren of Lindisfarne went with him to help him build his cell. They made it of stones they found on the island, and logs of wood, and rubble and clay. It was round in shape, and the wall was so high that a person inside could see nothing but the sky above him.

Near the place where they had landed they built a house called the Hospice, where visitors could stay, for although Cuthbert was going to be a hermit he was not allowed to cut himself off altogether from the monks on Lindisfarne, who might want his advice. While they were building the Hospice they found a fine spring of water.

They knew now that it would be possible to live there, if they could also grow some wheat.

Cuthbert had brought some seeds with him, which he sowed at the right season, and he waited through the winter to see if they would come up. But when spring came there was not a stalk or a leaf to be seen. He was very disappointed, but he would try again. If wheat would not grow, he thought, perhaps barley would; so he

He could spend his days in work and prayer

asked the monks for some barley seed and, though it was past the proper time for sowing, he put it in at once. Almost immediately a good crop sprang up, which made him very thankful and happy. He could live there now quite alone, growing his own food, without depending on anyone, and he could spend his days in work and prayer.

In the first year he was there, however, his plans were nearly ruined by the birds. They destroyed his crop of barley, and they pecked at the other things he had sown. There were in particular two crows who started to line their nests with the straw which made the thatch of the Hospice. Other birds followed their example, and the Hospice roof practically disappeared. Cuthbert decided that this was unfair on any monks who might come over as visitors, so he solemnly sent the two crows away, telling them not to come back.

For a time no more was seen of them. Then one day, when Cuthbert was digging his field, one of them came back. With his wings drooping and his head held down, he croaked at Cuthbert, and seemed to be asking for forgiveness. Cuthbert nodded at him in a friendly way. The crow seemed to understand, quickly flew off, and came back with the other crow. They then flew round and round the Saint, cawing happily, and one of them dropped from his beak a large lump of pig's lard, which Cuthbert found very useful for greasing his boots to keep out the wet. He and the crows became friendly, and they soon learnt not to spoil his crop of barley and steal the straw on the Hospice roof.

So at last everything was all right, and Cuthbert could lead the lonely life he had so long wanted to lead. He hoped he would be able to stay on Farne till he died, but one day the King himself, with many of his nobles, and the Bishop, came over to the little island, and, when they got to Cuthbert's cell, knelt down together and begged him to come back and be made Bishop of Lindisfarne. Because Cuthbert saw that that was what God wanted him to do, he did as they asked, and came back to fill the place once filled by that St Aidan whose soul he had seen being carried to Heaven on that night, long before, when he had been a shepherd on the hill-side.

XVII

ST GILES

GILES lived alone in a cave deep in a wild forest, not far from where the river Rhône flows into the Mediterranean Sea. He had, after many travels, made his home there so that he might escape from people who thought he was a saint. One day, as he was going into church, he had noticed a poor, sick beggar lying on the pavement outside; and to make him more comfortable he had taken off his own cloak and spread it over him. The man had been immediately healed, and the crowds started to gather and call Giles a holy man.

But Giles knew that the healing had nothing to do with his own goodness. He remembered, too, that when the people had surrounded Jesus after He had performed one of His miracles He had escaped from them and gone away alone into a deserted place to pray to God. Giles determined to try to do the same, not because he did not want to help the sick and the suffering, but because he thought the best way to do it was by hiding himself from the world and spending his time in prayer for it.

So he became a hermit in the forest of Nimes; and no one knew of his cave by the side of a clear spring, which gave him water to drink, as the trees and plants round about gave him herbs and fruits to eat. But he had one companion, a little hind who had become tame and made her home with him.

One day, when the King of that part of France was hunting in the Forest, the hind was pursued by the huntsmen and dogs, and in terror it fled to the cave and took refuge in Giles's arms. The prayers of the holy man—so the story says—caused thick bushes to spring up as a protection, so that the hounds were baffled. But one of the huntsmen shot an arrow in the direction the hind had taken, and when at last they found their way to the cave they discovered that the arrow had wounded, not the hind, but Giles.

When they saw this the King and his huntsmen were very sorry. They knelt and asked the hermit's forgiveness; but Giles, who realized it was an accident, said there was nothing to forgive. They offered to bind the wound; but Giles explained that it was of no account. The King implored him to come with him to court; but Giles told him that nothing would make him leave the way of life that he had chosen for the glory of God. So at last they left him alone and returned to the chase.

But now that he had discovered so famous a holy man living in his dominions the King could not let the matter rest. He went back to Giles and asked that, if he would not come to court, at least he would allow some people who were also trying to live a good life to come and live near him. Giles realized that this was his duty to God. About a hundred and fifty years earlier, you remember, St Benedict had gone away to serve God in the desert just as Giles had; but in the end he had allowed others who wished to serve God in the same way to come and live with him under a strict Rule of Life which he drew up for them. By Giles's day there were many monasteries in Europe under this Benedictine Rule; and Giles, after much prayer and thought, told the King that if he would build a Benedictine monastery near his cave he would become abbot of it.

This the King did; and though Giles himself never left his cave and at last died in it, the great Abbey of St Giles which was built there in the forest became one of the greatest homes of monks in France.

In France, in Italy, and in England, for the next hundred years or so, the Church was left in peace; but in Spain a new danger appeared which, in one form or

The King and the huntsman found Giles

another, was to attack Christendom for nearly a thousand years—the Mohammedans. And another land was added to Christendom, the land we now call Germany.

XVIII

ST BONIFACE

(ST BONIFACE'S DAY: JUNE 5)

ST BONIFACE, who is known as 'the Apostle of Germany,' was born at Crediton, in Devonshire, about 680, while St Giles was still alive. His English name was Winfred, and when he was five he was sent to school at the Benedictine monastery at Exeter. It was just at that time that all England finally became Christian, and as Winfred grew up he determined to become a missionary to Germany, the land of his ancestors, where the old gods, Odin and Thor, were still worshipped.

But before he could do this there was much learning to be done. He became a monk, was made head of an abbey school not far from Winchester, which was then the capital of England, and when he was thirty-six he set sail on his first mission with two or three companions in a German trading-vessel which he found on a visit to the little port of London.

When he arrived across the North Sea, among the sandy marshes and deep forests of Friesland, he found that things were not at all what he expected. A war had just broken out between the people of Friesland and the Franks (or, as we should call them to-day, the French) under their soldier-leader, Charles Martel. And Charles Martel and his people were Christians. Boniface soon found that as long as the Christian Charles Martel was striking down the German pagans with his battleaxe they were not going to pay any attention to him, a poor wandering monk, who was telling them that they must give up their warlike ways and bow down to the Cross of

Christ. So he returned to England to think out the best way to deal with the situation.

The next time he set out it was not to Germany he went but to Rome, to put the matter before the Pope and ask him what he should do. The Pope sent him to Germany again, as he asked to be sent, to make a report on the country and to see how it could best be made Christian. Boniface crossed the Alps and so came first to the south of Germany—to Bavaria and, going northward, to Thuringia, where once Christianity had been known—and by the time that he arrived back in Friesland, on the borders of the North Sea, everything had changed. Charles Martel had won his battles, the pagan duke of the Frisians was dead, and Christianity was already proclaimed the religion of the land. In those days a country had the same religion as its ruler, and as Charles Martel was a Christian, the Frisians were called Christians.

But really the people secretly, and in many places openly, still worshipped the old gods. Boniface sent for helpers from among his friends in England, and they went about the country founding monasteries and nunneries which should be centres of teaching for the pagans round about. The Pope made him the first 'Bishop of All Germany,' and Charles Martel saw to it that he was protected. For, as Boniface explained to his friend the Bishop of Winchester, without Charles's help he could neither defend his monks nor prevent idolatry. But he himself went about all the time, risking his own life to preach the Gospel and to try to make the Germans Christian at heart.

One of the sacred places of the heathen Germans was near Geismar, where there was an enormous oak-tree called 'Thor's Oak.' Boniface called together all the people of the neighbourhood who he knew still met there in the dead of night to worship Thor. Then when they were assembled—"a great crowd of pagans bitterly

cursing in their hearts this enemy of their gods,'' as the
old chronicler describes them—Boniface took an axe and
cut a notch at the base of the tree, calling on them to
watch how little sacred the oak was. "But when he had
made a superficial cut, suddenly the oak's vast bulk,
shaken by a mighty blast of wind, crashed to the ground,
shivering its topmost branches into fragments in its fall;
as if by the express will of God, for the monks present had

Many of the heathen were converted on the spot

done nothing to cause it." Many of the heathen there
who had expected Thor to strike Boniface dead with a
thunderbolt were converted on the spot and helped Boniface and the monks to build, from the timber of the oak,
a little chapel which was dedicated to St Peter.

Boniface continued his work of conversion till he was
over seventy, when at last he was martyred by an armed
band of still heathen Germans on the borders of Friesland. He had appointed a day when all those who had
recently been baptized should come together so that he,

as their Bishop, could confirm them. No sooner had they gathered than a great number of pagans, armed with spears and shields, rushed upon them. Boniface's attendants wanted to stand and fight, but he, perhaps remembering those long-ago days when fighting had prevented him making any converts, said: "Lay down your arms, for we are told in Scripture not to render evil for evil but to overcome evil by good. Endure with steadfast mind the sudden onslaught of death that you may be able to reign evermore with Christ." While he was speaking the enemy rushed on the Christians and killed them. When, after they had gone, Boniface's body was found he was still holding the book he had been reading—St Ambrose's *How to die well.*

Boniface was first buried in his cathedral at Mainz, but later men remembered that when he was alive he had said he wished to be buried in the Abbey of Fulda, which he had built at the beginning of his missionary work, so they reburied the body there.

Germany was now added to the lands of the Cross: but in Spain the battle was raging.

XIX

ST EULOGIUS OF CORDOVA

(ST EULOGIUS'S DAY: MARCH 11)

AFTER Arianism was beaten, the next great threat to the Christian faith came from the followers of Mohammed, whose new religion quickly swept over Africa and before long attacked Spain. The fierce Moorish warriors crossed by the Strait of Gibraltar and swarmed over the land, and eighty years after St Isidore's death they had conquered it all, except for the northern kingdoms. The Moors were not entirely driven out from Spain for eight hundred years.

When Eulogius was born, about the year 819, in the city of Cordova, where his family had been nobles since Roman times, the Moors had complete power there. They still allowed Christians to worship and hold their services as long as they paid heavy fines and did not try to make converts; and it seems that Eulogius was sent to be trained as a priest in the northern part of the country, where the Christians were still unconquered. But he came back to Cordova and was ministering to the Christians in his native city about the year 850, which was the beginning of what is now called 'the epoch of martyrs.'

In that year the Mohammedan rulers decided to begin a persecution of the Christians and try to stamp them out. Like the pagan Roman Emperors, they inflicted the death-sentence on anyone who became a convert or on any Christian who made a convert. Within three years twenty-five leading Christians in the city had been martyred, and the persecution had spread throughout the entire province. As in all such persecutions many of

72

the more timid Christians denied their faith, and Eulogius set himself the task of comforting them and encouraging them to stand firm: he wrote accounts of those who had bravely gone to death so that their examples would help the weaker ones. His book was called *The Memorial of the Saints.*

There was living in Cordova a Moorish girl named Leocritia who had been converted to Christianity. The

He took her to his sister, hoping she would be safe there

Moorish officers were coming to arrest her when she ran to Eulogius to ask if he would protect her. As he knew that the first place to be searched would be his own house, he took her to his sister, Annulona, hoping that she would be safe there. But the Moors heard of it, and they escaped only just before the soldiers called. Eulogius then took her to another Christian household, then again to another. All the time the officers were in pursuit and it was clear that Leocritia could not escape for long. Both she and Eulogius were captured and taken to immediate trial. Every one knew what the result would be: both were condemned to death and executed. Eulogius was martyred on Saturday, March 11, 859. The Moors hoped that once her teacher and protector was dead Leocritia would be frightened and return to their religion. But nothing would move her and she was beheaded on the following Wednesday, following Eulogius's example and protesting to the end her belief in Jesus Christ.

XX

ST SWITHUN

(ST SWITHUN'S DAY: JULY 15)

EGBERT, the King of the West Saxons who became the first King of England, took great care in finding the best person he could to bring up and teach his son, Ethelwulf. The man he chose was named Swithun, and when Ethelwulf grew up and himself became King he made his tutor Swithun the Bishop of Winchester. As Winchester was then the capital of England, this was a very important post. The King wanted to have Swithun near him so that he could advise him on how to govern the kingdom. And, because he knew how well Swithun had taught him when he was a boy, he asked the Bishop to look after *his* son too. That son was to be the most famous of all the Saxon kings—Alfred the Great.

Swithun's chief work, of course, was to rule the Church in the diocese of Winchester. When he was made Bishop the first thing he did was to travel all round it. So that there should be no great ceremony, he used to make his journeys on foot, and by night. One of the things he discovered was that many of his journeys took twice as long as they ought to have done because there were no proper bridges across some of the rivers. So, besides seeing that churches were built, he also had many bridges built.

One day, when Swithun was watching the workmen at work on a bridge at Winchester itself, he saw a poor woman carrying a basket of eggs to market. One of the men stumbled against her, and all the eggs were broken. The man took no notice of her when she complained.

"Look here," he said, "we're busy here on a great bridge. The Bishop himself's come to watch it. If you

75

get in the way of the work you must expect to get your eggs broken. And, anyway, what's a few eggs?"

It was the Bishop himself who answered.

"As much to this poor woman," he said, "as the bridge is to you and me."

"I was going to sell them in the market," said the woman. "And now I don't know what I shall do for the money."

No sooner did they start to dig than it started to rain

"You shall have your eggs," said Swithun. And, so the story says, he blessed the broken eggs, and they were made whole and sound.

Although Swithun had so much to do with the King and the princes, he loved most being among the simple people he met in his travels, and he ordered that when he died he should be buried outside the Cathedral where people would walk over his grave. But when he was dead the monks thought that such a grave was not fitting for so great a bishop. They obeyed his wishes by burying him outside the Cathedral, but they intended to remove the body almost immediately to a great shrine inside.

The day came when everything was ready to take the body out of the simple grave in the churchyard and carry it to the splendid tomb in the Cathedral. But no sooner did they start to dig than it started to rain. It was not just a shower, but such a torrent of rain that they could not go on with the work.

"Never mind," they said. "We will do it to-morrow."

But the next day it rained again in the same way. And the next. And the next. So at last they saw that they must obey Swithun's wish, and his body was left in the simple grave outside the Cathedral for more than a hundred years. Though it was then moved into the great shrine, people never forgot the rain-storms, and still to-day there is the saying that if it rains on St Swithun's Day there will be rain for forty days after.

XXI

ST WENCESLAUS

EVERY one knows how
Good King Wenceslaus looked out
On the Feast of Stephen

though probably few could say anything more about the king than the story of the carol. But that, perhaps, does not matter very much as long as he is thought of as 'good' King Wenceslaus. That was how men thought of him at the time, just as they thought of his twin brother as 'bad King Boleslaus.'

The story really begins with his grandmother, Ludmilla, who brought him up and who also was a saint. She was the wife of a Duke of Bohemia, in the south of Germany, and she and her husband were both converted to Christianity about a hundred years after Boniface died. Some say they were converted by monks from England, who were carrying on Boniface's work. Ludmilla brought up her son as a Christian, and in time, on his father's death, he became Duke of Bohemia and married a princess named Drahomira, who pretended to be a Christian but secretly was still a pagan and wanted to turn all Bohemia pagan again. They had twin children, Wenceslaus and Boleslaus, who were eight years old when their father died in 918. Wenceslaus who, as the elder, now became Duke, was sent just before his father's death to be brought up by his grandmother, St Ludmilla; while Boleslaus remained with his mother, Drahomira, who made him a pagan like herself.

As the boys grew up it became quite clear that there

would be a clash between them. Drahomira was supported by the pagan party, but the people so loved Ludmilla, who was the protectress of the Christians, that Drahomira was unable to do anything against her. And more and more people began to see that Wenceslaus was turning into a mild, merciful, and just young man who would be an admirable ruler, while Boleslaus was

At the church door he was murdered by his brother

fierce, cruel, and treacherous, and entirely under his mother's influence.

At last Drahomira decided to have Ludmilla murdered. She found two of her courtiers, who were great worshippers of the pagan gods and looked on the Christians with hatred, to undertake it. They went to Ludmilla's palace, where they found her kneeling at her prayers before a cross in her private chapel. They crept up behind her and strangled her with her own veil.

Wenceslaus, when his grandmother was dead—though he did not know then that it was his mother who had had her murdered—realized that the pagan forces were too strong for him to face alone. He put Bohemia under the direct protection of the Emperor, who gave him the title of King, and provided him with monks and priests from other parts of his German dominions to help to strengthen the Christians in Bohemia. He also granted Wenceslaus the right to carry on his shield and standard the black Imperial eagle when he found at last that he had to fight to save the Faith in his land.

In the battle which he fought against the pagans King Wenceslaus was victorious, and some men said that they saw two angels guarding him through the fiercest of the conflict. But before it was over the angels had left him, and the superstitious feared that the King was killed.

Wenceslaus, however, was still alive, though he was in deadly danger. After the battle his mother, Drahomira, asked him to come and visit her to talk matters over. The King, even though by now he knew her wickedness, was still an obedient son and went at her bidding to Bunzlau, where she was. As he entered the town he went first to the church there to pray, but at the church door he was murdered by his brother, Boleslaus, and his body hacked to pieces.

Three years after the murder Boleslaus repented of his awful deed, and had Wenceslaus reburied in the great church at Prague, the capital of Bohemia, and himself renounced his paganism. By his death, indeed, Wenceslaus did what in his lifetime he had never been able to do—made Bohemia Christian. And within thirty years of his martyrdom the Faith was so strong that Wenceslaus's friend, the Emperor Otto, gave Bohemia a bishop of its own with his seat in the Cathedral of Prague, where the good King lay in a shrine to which pilgrims came from all over Germany.

XXII

ST WOLFGANG

(ST WOLFGANG'S DAY: OCTOBER 31)

WHILE Wenceslaus was trying to make his part of the country Christian another saint, St Ulrich, was Bishop of Augsburg, about two hundred miles to the south-west. He, like Wenceslaus, was a great friend of the Emperor Otto, and his work was in making the Church in Germany stronger by building churches and monasteries, and seeing that the Christian priests and monks were really good and learned men whose lives were examples to all the people round about.

Then suddenly, in the year 955, a new horde of heathen barbarians, the Magyars from the Ural Mountains on the borders of Europe and Asia far away to the east, swept over the great plains, entered Germany, and, plundering and burning as they went, advanced right up to the gates of Augsburg itself. They besieged the city, and would have taken it had it not been for the leadership and courage of Ulrich, who inspired the people to hold out until the Emperor Otto, with his army, could come to their aid. At the great battle of the Lechfeld, near Augsburg, the Emperor finally defeated them and drove them back to the part of Europe we now call Hungary. Here they settled, and as long as they remained heathen they were a constant danger to Christian Germany.

So Ulrich and the Emperor determined that missionaries must be sent to preach the Gospel to them, and the man they chose for this dangerous task was Wolfgang, a young Benedictine monk who was already famous as a teacher. Ever since he was a small boy Wolfgang, who

81

belonged to the family of the Counts of Swabia, had wanted to learn as much as he could. He had visited the great monasteries, which were the schools and universities of those days, to attend lectures by teachers from Italy and France; and now he was grown up what he wanted most of all was himself to teach others. But he had not thought of being sent to preach the Gospel simply to warlike barbarians who had never heard of Christ. Nevertheless, as soon as St Ulrich, who had ordained him a priest, told him what was wanted he did not hesitate, but left the abbey where he was happy teaching and went as a missionary to the Magyars.

He was so successful that within a year or two many other missionaries, including a bishop, were sent to help him, and he himself was recalled to Germany and made Bishop of Ratisbon. Here, at last, he was able to have a special school, and among his pupils was Henry, the young Duke of Bavaria who was later to become Emperor and ruler of Germany.

One day, when Wolfgang was visiting some of the abbeys under his charge to see that everything was in good order, he came to the edge of a great forest. Suddenly he thought that perhaps it was God's will that he should end his days as a hermit, living alone, saying his prayers, far away from other men. His work seemed done. He had learnt and taught; he had converted the heathen, and seen that all things were properly ordered in his diocese; he had advised the Emperor when, as a Prince of the Empire, it had been his duty to do so. Now he would go into the forest and be alone with God until death. Taking with him only an axe with which he could cut down a tree to make himself a little hut, he went into the deserted forest and found a thicket by a stream, where he knelt down and prayed. Then he threw his axe as far as he could, and where it fell he regarded as the place where God intended him to build his cell.

How long he lived there the story does not tell; but one day a hunter discovered him and, finding out who he was and knowing how worried every one was at his mysterious disappearance, persuaded him to return to Ratisbon and take up his work again. In later days a small town, which was named St Wolfgang, sprang up

He would go into the forest and be alone with God until death

where his cell had been, and here people could still, even in this century, see the axe which always appears in paintings of the saint.

Wolfgang died in the year 994 when he was travelling down the Danube to visit some monasteries in the south of Germany, and his body was taken to be buried in the great Abbey of St Emmerman where much of his work had been done.

XXIII

ST HENRY AND ST CUNEGUND

(ST HENRY'S DAY: JULY 15; ST CUNEGUND'S DAY: MARCH 3)

HENRY, the young Duke of Bavaria who had been taught by St Wolfgang, became ruler of Germany in the year 1002, when he was thirty years old. He married the beautiful daughter of the Count of Luxembourg, Cunegund, and together husband and wife determined to give an example of Christian rulers of a Christian country. It was now 250 years since St Boniface had died, and, though there were still some heathens against whom Henry had to fight—the Prussians in the north and the Saracens in Italy in the south—his main work was to carry on the pattern which had been set by Boniface and Charles Martel and continued by Ulrich, Wolfgang, and other great bishops working with Otto the Great. The churchmen and the kings had helped each other to make a Christian Church in a Christian State; and now Henry, himself the head of the State but brought up by St Wolfgang, was to carry on the work of them all and to be the first of the Emperor-Saints.

There were times, however, when he became very tired of ruling and fighting, and wished that he could give it all up and become a simple monk. During every journey and campaign, whenever he entered a town or city for the first time, he would go immediately to say his prayers in a church dedicated to the Blessed Virgin Mary, to whom he had always had a particular devotion.

Once he was praying this way in the Abbey of Verdun, when he made up his mind that he would have nothing more to do with the pomp and cares of his position, and

84

would really take the step of becoming a monk. He had talked over the matter with Cunegund and, as they had no children, she was content for him to do it, because she herself would then become a nun; and as they loved each other very dearly, they knew they would still be close to each other in the love of God. So Henry went to the Abbot and told him that he wished to give up his crown and become an ordinary monk in the Benedictine Order.

"I order you to carry out the duties which God gave you"

"The first vow you will have to take," said the Abbot, "is the vow of obedience."

"I am quite ready to obey whatever you, as my religious superior, would tell me to do," said Henry.

"Then," said the Abbot, "I order you to carry out the duties which God gave you. He made you Emperor, and you show your obedience to Him by ruling wisely and doing His will in the state of life He called you to."

So Henry went back to his capital and continued his reign.

One of the things that caused him most sorrow was the way in which some of the nobles blamed him for his love of religion. They thought the money he spent on building churches, especially the cathedral at Bamberg which he made one of the most beautiful in Europe at that time, could have been better spent in the interests of the court and the courtiers.

When Henry reproved them they took their revenge by making up false tales about Cunegund and spreading them round the court. Though both Henry and Cunegund knew they were lies, so many people came to believe them, and to say that the Empress was only pretending to be good but had really committed various crimes, that they felt something must be done. So Cunegund said that, before them all, she would submit to the ordeal which in those days was sometimes used instead of a trial. The accused persons had to walk barefoot over red-hot ploughshares, and if they were innocent God would, so people thought, prevent them being hurt, just as in the Old Testament story He had protected the young men in the burning fiery furnace.

Cunegund not only walked this path of fire without any hurt, but she actually carried a ploughshare in her hand.

After Henry died Cunegund became a nun, and spent the rest of her life doing good to all who needed it. Of all the nuns in her convent she was the most industrious; and when people said that it was strange that one who had been an Empress should work so hard she told them that she and Henry had always, in the sphere in which God had set them, worked as hard as they could for His glory. And long after she was dead the young nuns remembered that she was always quoting the words of St Paul—that those who did not work had no right to eat.

Henry and Cunegund were buried side by side in their Cathedral of Bamberg, where they still lie in the tomb that was made for them then, and where, from the sculptures of them, you can still see what they looked like. And in paintings of the saints you can easily recognize them because St Henry, wearing his Imperial crown and robes, holds in one hand the orb, representing the rulership to which he returned because of his obedience, and in the other a model of Bamberg Cathedral; and St Cunegund is shown walking on the ploughshares, holding another ploughshare in her hand.

Four years after her death in Germany a prince who was to become a saint was made King of England.

XXIV

ST EDWARD THE CONFESSOR

(ST EDWARD THE CONFESSOR'S DAY: OCTOBER 13)

EDWARD was born at Islip, near Oxford. He was the son of that King Ethelred who is called 'the Unready,' who ruled so unwisely that the Danes managed to conquer England and become kings of it. Little Edward's mother, after Ethelred died, married again—the Danish King Canute—and in the wars and civil wars of those days Edward was sent for safety into France, and was brought up at the Norman court.

It was not till he was nearly forty that, as the other royal princes and the Danes who wanted the crown of England had died or been murdered, Edward was sent for to become King of England. He was a tall, gentle man, who was fond of hunting and hawking and outdoor sports of all kinds as well as of books and learning; but, above all, he tried to live the kind of life which he knew Christ would wish. He could not, of course, become a monk, because he knew that it was his duty one day to be King; but, he determined, if ever he was called back to England he would try to be a 'father to his people' and show what a Christian king could be; and in a land where, for years, they had been fighting and murdering for power and money, they should have a king who cared for neither.

When he became King he found that most of his own money came from a tax called the Danegeld which his father, many years ago, had made people pay so that he could give it to the Danes to stop them attacking him. There had been no need for the tax for a long time, because the Danes had actually been ruling England, but those in power went on collecting it, and making the poor people pay it. The year that Edward came back they made a special effort to get as much money as they could. They thought the new King would be pleased, and reward them for it. So the chief noble took Edward into a room of the palace where a great heap of gold pieces were lying.

"That, your Majesty, is the money we have collected for you," he said. "You will be pleased that it's a bigger amount this year than it has ever been."

"Where does it come from?" asked the King.

"The people."

"The poor people?"

"Some of them are poor, yes. But they all pay the tax so that the land shall be protected."

"But," said the King, "there is no enemy now for them to be protected from. In my father's time this money was not kept by him. It was paid to the Danes. I shall not keep it either."

"What will you do with it, your Majesty?" asked the nobles.

"Give it back to the people you stole it from," said the King. "See that it is all returned to the poor from whom it was taken."

When Edward had been in exile in Normandy he had made a vow that, if he ever came back to the throne of England, he would make a pilgrimage to Rome; and he started putting his own money aside to pay for this. But, as he saw how difficult it was to rule the country, he started to wonder whether it would be wise for the King to be away for such a long time as the pilgrimage would take. So he sent to the Pope to ask if he might be allowed not to fulfil his vow.

The Pope said he could be excused from coming to Rome on one condition—that he would spend the money he had saved and any more he might raise to building a great church in his capital dedicated to St Peter. This Edward was only too delighted to do, and he spent much money and time and thought on it. And that is how Westminster Abbey came to be built, where to-day at the very centre of it St Edward lies buried in his shrine.

One day, early in his reign, he was present at the dedication of another church, which had just been built in Essex in honour of St John the Evangelist. An old

He took a gold ring from his finger and gave it to the old man

beggar came up to him and asked him for alms. Edward (as was usually the case) had no money with him, but he immediately took a gold ring from his finger and gave it to the old man, who thanked him and went away. Many years later some English pilgrims in Jerusalem met the same beggar, who explained to them that he was St John the Evangelist, and had come to the opening of the church built in his honour, and that he wanted them to take the ring back to King Edward with the message that within six months he would die and be taken to Heaven.

They brought the ring back to the King, who immediately recognized it, and who began to prepare himself for death. He lived just long enough to know that the building of his great church at Westminster was finished, though he was too ill to be at the opening of it, and he was the first person to be buried there. In pictures of St Edward the Confessor, in books or in stained-glass windows, he is usually shown holding the ring which was sent back to him in such a miraculous way.

Before he died he warned the courtiers and nobles round him that their wickedness would bring great trouble on the country. In that same year, 1066, England was conquered by the Normans, and the ordinary people, oppressed and killed once more, mourned for the days of 'good King Edward.'

XXV

ST BENNO

IN the same year—1066—a nobleman named Benno was made Bishop of Meissen, in Saxony. The Emperor of Germany at that time, Henry IV, was a boy of sixteen, and he was a very different kind of person from St Henry II, who had always tried to rule the State or the good of religion and the Church. Henry IV, on the other hand, intended to try to make the Church obey the State, and one of his plans was to make the German bishops entirely dependent on him. He, and not the Pope, gave to each newly made bishop the crozier and the ring which showed his 'marriage' to the Church.

But it happened that at that time there was one of the greatest of the Popes, St Gregory VII, who was equally determined that the Emperor should do nothing of the kind; and this led to the long struggle you read about in your history books. It was called the 'Investiture Contest,' and went on for many years all over Europe to decide whether the Pope, as Head of the Church, or the ruler of the State should 'invest' bishops with the symbols of their holy office.

The reason St Benno is important among the saints of Germany is because, unlike some of the German bishops, he stood out against the Emperor, and because not even imprisonment could make him say that Henry was right. We do not know very much about his life, apart from the warfare and struggles of the time. But there is one story which has become famous. When the Pope had said that the Emperor, because he would not obey the Church, was not to be allowed to receive Holy

Communion Henry hoped that the German bishops would take no notice of this 'excommunication.' He rode with his followers to Meissen and demanded entry to the cathedral. Benno realized that there was nothing he could do to keep him out unless he shut the cathedral to every one, so he ordered everything to be fastened up from the inside and then the great door locked on the outside. When this had been done, in front of all the people, he threw the key far out into the river Elbe.

He shut the Cathedral to every one

Henry knew that if he gave his soldiers orders to break down the door he would have every one against him, so he rode away, vowing vengeance on the Bishop. When he had gone the question was how the cathedral could be opened again. Benno, after much prayer, told a fisherman to throw his net into the river as near as he could to where the key had fallen, and, so the story says, among the fish that were caught that day was one which had the key hanging on to one of its fins. So, among the paintings of the saints which you can see to-day, you can always recognize St Benno, because he is holding a fish and a key.

He lived to be a very old man (some say that he was nearly a hundred when he died), and at the end of his life he followed the example of so many of the German saints and went to preach to the barbarians on the outskirts of the country who were still heathen. He was buried in his cathedral at Meissen, but when, at the time of the German Reformation, four hundred years later, the countryside left the Catholic Church and became Protestant his body was removed, for safety, to Munich, and from that time St Benno has been considered the Patron Saint of that city.

XXVI

ST GREGORY THE SEVENTH

(ST GREGORY VII's DAY: MAY 25)

THE Pope of the 'Investiture Contest,' Gregory VII, like Gregory the Great, five hundred years earlier, was also a monk in a Benedictine monastery, and was called upon to defend the Church. His name was Hildebrand, and he was the son of a carpenter of Sovana. He was not very tall; he spoke with a stammer; and the only remarkable thing people could see about him was his glittering bright eyes which made them say that he was like his name, which means 'a bright flame.'

The times in which he lived were bad ones for the Church. People said that it seemed as if Christ were asleep and His vessel, the Church, tossed about at the mercy of the storm. One man wrote, "The whole world lay in wickedness; holiness had disappeared; justice had perished; and truth had been buried." The worst of it was that the wickedness of the world had got inside the Church itself. Monasteries had fallen into ruin; priests no longer looked after their people; bishops only cared for money and land and luxury.

Hildebrand saw that one of the reasons for this was that the kings and princes of Europe insisted that every bishop should pay homage to them, just as if they were ordinary nobles. They, and not the Pope or his representatives, gave the new bishop the crozier—the 'shepherd's crook,' which showed that he was to obey Jesus's command, "Feed my sheep"—and the ring, which showed his 'marriage' to the Church. These things, of course, should never have been given by anyone who was not himself a representative of Christ's Church; but the kings and princes refused to give up the right of 'investiture,' as it was called. So the wrong kind of men became bishops, and the whole Church suffered.

When Hildebrand became Pope he said that this must stop. He turned out the bishops who had allowed a layman to 'invest' them, and he said that any ruler who continued to do this should not be allowed to take Holy Communion. Even the most powerful of all the rulers, Henry, the Emperor, who ruled over what is now Germany and parts of Italy, was excommunicated. When Henry prepared to fight rather than obey, the Pope pronounced him deposed. "For the honour and security of the Church, in the name of God Almighty, I prohibit Henry, who has risen against the Church, from ruling Germany and Italy. I release all Christians from the oaths of fealty they may have taken to him, and I order that no one shall obey him."

At first Henry did not take much notice, but when some of his own people like St Benno were turning against him in Germany he thought he had better make friends with the Pope and get him to forgive him. So he set out on a journey to Italy, secretly hoping that, even if the Pope remained hard, some Italians would come over to his side.

It was in the middle of winter, and Gregory was in a castle called Canossa, far up in the mountains. Henry, finding that the Italians would not fight for him, made the long journey there through the snow. But when he arrived the Pope refused to see him.

"If the King is truly sorry," he said, "let him surrender his crown and sceptre to me to prove it."

But in the end he allowed Henry, after he had kept him waiting in the castle yard for three days, barefoot, fasting, and clothed like a penitent, to see him.

Henry threw himself at Gregory's feet, crying, "Holy Father, spare me," and was immediately forgiven.

Gregory had insisted on this, not, of course, because he did not like Henry, but because he wanted to give every one in Europe a lesson that the power of the Church, because it is founded by Christ, is more important than any earthly power at all. And in your history books you will still read about Canossa, which happened just eleven years after the battle of Hastings

Henry threw himself at Gregory's feet

was won in England by one of Gregory's friends, William the Conqueror.

Though Henry pretended to be sorry, he was not so really. He went away again, broke all his promises, raised a great army, and drove Gregory out of Rome.

The Saint's last words as he died in exile at Spoleto were, "Because I have loved righteousness and hated iniquity, therefore I die in exile." But in the years to come it was his cause, not Henry's, which was victorious.

XXVII

ST NORBERT

(ST NORBERT'S DAY: JUNE 6)

NORBERT, the son of one of the German counts and a relative of the Emperor, was born in Xanten, on the Rhine, in the year 1080. When he was quite young he was given a post at the court of the Emperor, Henry V (whose wife, Matilda, later tried to get the throne of England from King Stephen, as you may remember from your history lessons). Norbert—rich, handsome, and clever—greatly enjoyed his life as a courtier and cared for nothing but pleasure. But one day when he was riding not far from Xanten he was caught in a sudden thunderstorm. A thunderbolt actually fell just in front of his horse, which reared and plunged in panic so that Norbert was thrown violently to the ground, and it was an hour before his attendants could restore him to consciousness. When he recovered his senses he was a changed man. He realized how near death he had been and what a careless, sinful life he had led, and he determined that the future should be quite different.

He placed himself under the guidance of a Benedictine abbot and became a priest. He celebrated his first Mass at Xanten, and at it he preached a sermon reminding men how short life is and how they owe it to God to live it as He wishes. Some of the worldly clergy there were so angry that, it is said, one even spat in his face afterwards. He was not angry with them, but he determined to show them that he himself was prepared to do what he asked other people to do. He sold all his great possessions and gave the money to the poor, keeping for himself only what was needed to celebrate Mass. With a mule to carry the vestments and the sacred vessels, he set out, clothed in a lamb-skin, with a cord round his waist, and barefoot, to go through Germany preaching repentance like a new St John the Baptist. He travelled in this way to France, where he turned men from their careless way of living, and to Italy, where he visited

There was a procession of white-robed men coming out of the Chapel

the Pope, who wished to keep him at his court. But Norbert would not stay—he was afraid of courts—so the Pope gave him permission to continue his preaching wherever in Europe he found need for it. He offered him the Bishopric of Cambrai, but Norbert refused it, because he was sure that he had other work to do for God.

One night he had a dream in which he saw a great meadow in the middle of a forest. In it was a ruined chapel, dedicated to St John the Baptist, and there was a

99

procession of white-robed men coming out of it. And it seemed that he was not there by chance but that the Blessed Virgin Mary was herself pointing it out to him. It was, indeed, a vision rather than a dream. Some time later as, with a few companions, he was travelling through the forest of Coucy, he suddenly came upon the spot which he had seen in that vision, and, going to pray in the little chapel, he knew what he had to do. He was to found a new Order in the Church, of men who, like himself, would live in poverty and holiness and call the careless to repentance. He named the place Prémontré, which means 'the meadow that was pointed out,' and his new Order, dressed in white woollen cloaks over coarse black habits like those he had seen, was called—as its members still are to-day—the Premonstratensians. At first he and his companions lived in huts of wood and clay, arranged like a camp round the little chapel, but they soon built a larger church and a monastery to house the people who soon began to join the new Order.

Norbert, as he was travelling to various places to get money and help for Prémontré, visited once more the Emperor's court, where some of his old friends remembered him. One of these companions of his youth, seeing him barefoot, ill-dressed, and worn with fasting, said: "Oh, Norbert! That I should live to see you like this!"

One of the young chaplains, named Hugh, was much surprised that the courtier should even recognize the beggar, and asked who he was.

"That," said the courtier, "was once the gayest and most carefree man at court. And if he is now poor and despised it is because he has refused wealth and honours. I have heard that the Bishopric of Cambrai was offered to him, but he would not take it."

Hugh, who was himself meaning to make a career at

court, was so impressed that he joined Norbert, went back with him to Prémontré, and became, in time, his second-in-command.

In the first five years after the founding of the new Order it spread over Europe. Houses were established in Germany and France, and in what are now Holland and Belgium. Norbert decided that he must get the new Pope's blessing on it and authority to continue it, so with Hugh and two other companions he set out for Rome once more. The new Pope confirmed the Order but at the same time gave Norbert other work to do. He was now forty-six years old, and, as the Investiture Contest was still continuing, the authorities in the Church felt the need of Norbert's power and intellect in ruling the German Church. So Norbert, though he did not wish it, was made Bishop of Magdeburg.

When he went to Magdeburg to be installed he travelled simply as he always did. He arrived at night when the gates were shut, and when, in answer to the knocking, the porter looked out to see who was there he called roughly: "Away, fellow—we don't want any beggars here." The porter, of course, apologized when he realized that the 'beggar' was the new Prince-Bishop; but there were others in Magdeburg who did not want any interference in their worldly life, such as they felt the saintly Norbert would insist on. And when as Bishop he tried to put things right and return to the poor and the Church the goods and land that had been taken by the powerful and rich men of Magdeburg, three attempts were made to murder him.

Norbert, now—at the end of his life as he had been at the beginning—frequently at court as the friend of the Emperor and of the Pope alike, made one last journey to Rome to reconcile them to each other, but his great labours had worn him out. He had to be carried in a litter to Magdeburg, where he died just after Whit-

Sunday in 1134 without being able to visit his beloved Prémontré again.

The effort of the monasteries to become what they were meant to be was made in France as well as in Germany.

XXVIII

ST BERNARD OF CLAIRVAUX

(ST BERNARD'S DAY: AUGUST 20)

ABOUT the year 1100 certain monks decided that they would try to live again strictly according to the old Rule, and they went off into a lonely place called Cîteaux to found a new monastery. They took their name from the place and were known as Cistercians; but the life they led was so hard that, one after another, the monks left, and it seemed that the monastery would have to close.

Then one evening in the year 1113, just as the monks were going to bed, there was a loud knocking at the gate. The Abbot, who was an Englishman named Stephen Harding, ordered it to be opened and saw standing there about thirty men. He did not know whether they were robbers or travellers.

"Do you come in peace?" he asked.

"The peace of God," answered the young man of twenty-two who seemed to be the leader.

"Then, you are welcome to stay here for the night."

"If you will have us, Father," said the young man, "we have come to stay for ever."

Then he explained that his name was Bernard, the son of the Lord of Fontaines, one of the leading nobles of Burgundy, and that with him were some of his five brothers and other relations as well as friends. They all wished to become monks at Cîteaux.

"My children," said the Abbot, "even if I could refuse you I would not, for this is the Lord's doing and marvellous in our eyes. You have come at a moment when I was near to despair. It seemed that we were defeated and that the world was laughing at us. And now God has sent you in answer to our prayers and faith. Yet I must warn you that life here in the service of God is a life of hardship, having little comfort, needing no less bravery than a soldier needs who faces the dangers of war."

"I know, and they know," said Bernard. "Many of them have been soldiers."

So Bernard and his companions put on the white robe of the Cistercians, and for two years they stayed at Cîteaux, until at the end of that time Abbot Stephen sent twelve of them under Bernard's leadership to found a new house. The place they chose was by a river in the woods, which was known as the Valley of Bitterness. With Bernard went his four brothers Gerard and Guy and Andrew and Bartholomew, his uncle Gauldry, and his young cousin Robert.

It was very hard work, for first they had to make a clearing in the woods before they could set up the first rough building, from which in time the monastery would grow. They cut down trees for timber; they made their bricks from clay they baked on the spot; and their roof was a thatch of rushes. They had taken with them a little supply of barley and millet, from which they made some coarse black bread; and they made soup of beech-leaves soaked in water with a little salt.

One day they found that they had hardly any bread left and no salt, so Bernard sent one of his brothers off to the nearest town to get some.

"Can I have some money to buy it with?" he asked.

"When have we ever had money since we left home?" said Bernard. "Go and ask in God's name, and in God's name it will be given you."

At the edge of the wood the brother met a priest, who asked him where he was going. On being told, the priest said that his people would be only too glad to help the monks, and at once sent over half a barrel of salt and plenty of bread for them all.

When at last the house was built Bernard changed the name of the place where it stood. Now it was no longer the Valley of Bitterness. It was the Valley of Light— Clairvaux. And that is why he is always known in history as Bernard of Clairvaux.

They built their own monastery

But soon Clairvaux was too small to hold all the people who came to it asking to be monks there. Bernard's own father was one of those who came. The monastery grew famous, and Bernard himself became the friend and adviser of kings and bishops. Once the Pope himself visited Clairvaux, but, although that was a very great occasion, the simple Rule was not altered. The best meal the monks could give him was bread and a few fish and, instead of wine, the juice of herbs.

Besides his work as an abbot and his preaching, Bernard was a great writer; and one of his Latin hymns, *Jesu dulcis memoria*, which in English begins, "Jesus, the very thought of Thee with sweetness fills my breast," is still sung all over the world.

XXIX

ST THOMAS OF CANTERBURY

(ST THOMAS OF CANTERBURY'S DAY: DECEMBER 29)

HENRY II became King of England when he was only twenty-one, so he chose the cleverest man in the kingdom to help him rule wisely. This man was named Thomas Becket. He was fifteen years older than the King, and he was glad to be able to help Henry to rule the land well. They became very great friends, and were always together. At that time there were many strong nobles who tried to take no notice of the King's law, but held little law-courts of their own, and Henry and Thomas were determined that this should stop. Every one, they said, must come under the royal justice.

When the Archbishop of Canterbury died Henry decided to make Thomas Archbishop in his place.

"No, no," said Thomas. "You must not do that."

"Why?" asked Henry. "You are my closest friend, and you will be able to bring the Church courts under the King's law. We have built up the law in this land— you and I. At the King's Courts men can have justice and safety once more. My judges cannot be frightened by force or bribed by gold. There is only one kind of court left which makes its own laws—the Church court. If I make you Archbishop you can see that that too obeys the King."

"No," said Thomas. "If you make me Archbishop my first duty will be to the Church. And that will be the end of our friendship."

But the King did not believe him. He was sure that Thomas would really do as he wanted, and he made him Archbishop, in spite of all his protests.

107

As soon as Thomas was consecrated Archbishop of Canterbury he became a different man. Instead of living a gay, extravagant life, he became quiet and humble. Instead of wearing rich clothes and jewels, he dressed like a monk and wore a hair-shirt next to his skin. Instead of giving the great feasts he once did, he lived on so little food that he might have been a hermit. And instead of helping the King to do away with the Church courts, he did what he had warned Henry he would do—upheld the Church in every way he could.

The Church courts were never allowed to condemn anyone to death, though if any cleric had committed some dreadful crime, such as murder, he could be turned out of the Church, and then the ordinary law-courts could try him. Henry wanted clerics to have to appear in the ordinary courts in the first place, but the Church said that priests and other people in orders ought to be tried by Church people and not by lay people. The Church, because it was specially founded by God, was more important than the State, and it was wrong of the King to try to put the State over it.

When Henry found that Thomas was against him he broke out into a terrible rage. He said he was ungrateful, because everything he had he owed to the King.

"Are you not the son of one of my poor subjects?" he asked.

"Certainly I am poorly born," answered Thomas. "I have no royal blood. But neither had St Peter, who was a fisherman, and to him our Lord gave the keys of the Kingdom of Heaven and the headship of the whole Church."

"True," said the King. "But he died for his Lord."

"And I," said the Archbishop, "will die for my Lord when the time comes."

It was some years before that time came. Many people tried to make Henry and Thomas friends again, but it was always impossible, because the only thing the King wanted was that the Archbishop should give way on the matter of the Church courts; and that was the one thing he would not do. When it was time for Henry's eldest son to be crowned to reign with his father—as was the custom in those days—the one person who should have put the crown on his head was the Archbishop of Canterbury. But Thomas was not in England, and thereupon, instead of waiting for him to come, the Archbishop of York and some other bishops performed the ceremony. When Thomas heard of it he excommunicated them—that is to say, he said they were no longer to be members of the Church.

The Archbishop of York, who was a particular enemy of Thomas's, complained to the King, "My lord, as long as Thomas lives, we shall have no peace or quiet."

Then the King broke out in one of his crazy rages. "Why am I troubled with this? Why cannot my servants deal with this turbulent priest? This fellow I loaded with benefits dares insult the King and the whole kingdom. What cowards have I in my Court who care nothing for the duty they owe me? Will no one deliver me from this low-born priest?"

There were four ruffians standing by as the King said this, and they determined to do a deed which they thought would bring them much money and thanks from Henry. On the afternoon of December 29, 1170, they called on the Archbishop in his palace at Canterbury, and threatened to kill him if he did not do as the King wished. They gave him a few hours to think it over, and said they would come back again at sunset.

"I shall be here," said Thomas.

The monks of Canterbury, who had found out what had happened, implored the Archbishop to fly to safety, but he would not. They asked him at least to go into the Cathedral, thinking that even the wicked knights

would not dare to attack him there. And, as he would
not do that either, they got hold of him by force, and in
spite of his resistance they pulled, dragged, and pushed
him, taking no notice of his orders to let him go, until
they got him into the sacred building. They asked him
to allow the doors to be bolted.

"It is not right to turn God's House into a fortress,"
said Thomas.

Then the four knights advanced to where he stood

"But, Father, look! There are four soldiers there with
drawn swords."

"God will protect His own," said Thomas. "We shall
win by suffering rather than by fighting."

Then suddenly out of the shadows of the Cathedral
came the voice of one of the knights, "Where is Thomas,
traitor to the King?"

"I am here," answered Thomas, "a priest of God."

"For the last time, in the King's name, we order you to
obey the King," shouted another of the knights.

"I cannot obey the King in things which he has no

right to ask. But I am ready to die," answered Thomas, "that with my blood the Church may obtain liberty and peace. But, in the name of Almighty God, I forbid you to hurt my people."

Then the four knights advanced to where he stood and murdered him there in his own Cathedral.

So St Thomas of Canterbury died, and, in dying, he won what he had been struggling for; for the King, horrified by the news, not only stopped all his attacks on the Church and the Church courts, but, so that the whole world might know how sorry he was, he allowed himself to be scourged at Thomas's tomb.

XXX

ST HILDEGARD

BOTH St Benno and St Norbert had to fight, in different ways, the evils that came on the Church in Germany, because some of the bishops and clergy forgot to put their duty to God first, and behaved like ordinary noblemen and their dependants in trying to get wealth and comfort and power. But it was a woman, Hildegard (who was born while St Norbert was still alive), who became so famous by her sermons and her prophecies in making them see how wrong they were that she is still known as the 'Sibyl of the Rhine.'

"Instead of being like the Apostles," she proclaimed, "you are so sunk in worldly indolence that your time is spent in waging wars, or with buffoons and singers. You ought to be pillars of the Church, learned in the Scriptures, filled with the Holy Spirit; but instead you are ruining the Church by your bad examples."

Hildegard's father was a soldier in the service of one of the German counts, and when she was eight years old she was placed in the care of the Count's sister, who was a Benedictine nun. Eventually Hildegard, who was not very strong and sometimes had spells of blindness, became a nun too. Even when she was still a girl she found that in her illnesses she would see and hear strange things. She thought of them as dreams until she found that, after she had told them to her nurses, some of them came true. "A great fear came over me," she wrote. "Frequently in my conversation I would talk of future things which I saw as if they were happening at the moment; but, noticing the amazement of my companions, I began not to talk about them."

Of course, people who had heard of Hildegard's visions began to discuss this strange nun, and at last her confessor told her that she must write some of them down so that they could be tested and an opinion formed on whether the visions really came from God or whether Hildegard was only a fraud. She was terrified of doing this but

Standing on the summit, she prayed for the Crusade

obeyed the order, and some time afterwards the writings were shown to the Pope himself. After a great deal of discussion and testing the Church pronounced that Hildegard had really been favoured by God with gifts of prophecy.

She left the convent where she had been brought up to found another near Bingen, on the Rhine. Here crowds of people came from all over Germany and France to hear her words of wisdom and to receive advice and help. Archbishops, abbots, nobles, and simple, ordinary people visited her, and among them was St Bernard of Clairvaux, who was trying to get Christians to stop fighting one another and band together in a Crusade to rescue the Holy Land from the Mohammedans. Hildegard helped him by her prayers. While he was preaching down by the river Rhine she went up to the Feldberg, the highest peak of the hills there, and, standing on its summit with her arms outstretched, she prayed for the Crusade. So long did she stay that at the end she fainted with tiredness.

Hildegard recorded many of her visions and much of her teaching in a book which took her ten years to write. It is one of the most famous books of the time and is known as the *Scivias* (a shortening of its full title, *Scire vias Domini*, which means 'Know the ways of the Lord'). One of the precious manuscript copies of it is in England, at the University of Oxford; and when, three hundred years after Hildegard's death, printing was invented the *Scivias* was one of the first books to be printed.

Not long before she died Hildegard's goodness was put to a severe test. In the cemetery next to her convent a young man had been buried. He had been excommunicated by one of the archbishops, and Hildegard was ordered to have his body dug up and buried somewhere else. But Hildegard knew that the young man, before he died, had been sorry for his sins and had made a confession of them and received the Holy Sacrament. She explained this to the authorities and said that, because of it, she could not obey them. It would, she said, be very wrong to do so. So, to punish her, she and the whole convent were not allowed to partake of Holy Communion, and special men were sent down to remove the body. But in the night Hildegard went into the cemetery and removed all traces of the grave, so that it could not be found by the men when they arrived. At last, after much trouble and by appealing to another archbishop, she managed to get the sentence against her convent and herself removed, and was given permission to leave the young man's body buried in consecrated ground. In this way she taught another lesson to the people of her time, who were surprised that so famous and holy a woman should bother about what might have seemed a very little thing.

XXXI

ST HUGH OF LINCOLN

(ST HUGH'S DAY: NOVEMBER 17)

ONE of the things King Henry II of England did to show he was sorry for St Thomas of Canterbury's death was to bring to England some monks from the famous French monastery of the Grande Chartreuse—the Great Charterhouse—who were called Carthusians, to strengthen the Church in England. He gave them some land at Witham, in Somerset, where there was a large forest, and they could build their house far away from the busy life of the world. At first they were not very successful. The Somerset people did not like them because they were foreigners, and would not help them in their building. They got cold and ill in their huts of mud and branches by the edge of the river. One of the Priors who looked after them died, and another went back to France. Then, when it seemed as if the plan would be a total failure, a monk named Hugh was sent to take charge.

Almost at once everything started to go right. Hugh won the love of the Somerset folk by his goodness and his sense of fun, which, since the days when he played pranks in his father's castle, he had never lost. He was himself very interested in building, and he designed, and helped to build with his own hands, a beautiful white-stoned church at the edge of the forest. The monks taught the children round about and cared for the sick and fed the poor, and the monastery at Witham became such a good and happy place that even the King used to go and stay there to get away from his unhappy Court with all its disputes and troubles.

It was not long before Henry decided that Hugh must become a bishop. The diocese of Lincoln, one of the largest in England, had had no bishop for eighteen years, and the clergy had fallen into bad ways because there was no one to look after them. Though Hugh wanted to stay at Witham, he at last consented to be made Bishop, and he set about putting things in order in Lincoln. He travelled all round the diocese on a horse, with a little

He travelled all round the diocese on a horse

bundle of his belongings strapped on to it. People thought that a bishop ought to travel about in a much grander manner, but Hugh refused to alter it; and as often as he could he went back to stay at Witham, where he had a cell alone in the forest. When he was at his bishop's manor at Stowe he had as a particular pet a great wild swan which was so fierce that it would let no one come near it; but with Hugh it was quite tame and ate out of his hand and went everywhere with him. It too was a creature of the forest.

At that time the King's Foresters were among the

worst people in the land. Because they were the King's own men they behaved as if they were a law to themselves, and took no notice of the law which Henry made every one else obey. One of the Foresters had behaved unjustly to one of the Bishop's men on the manor of Stowe, and Hugh excommunicated him. Henry immediately ordered Hugh to appear before him and answer for his action. He said he had no right to do it.

Hugh immediately went into the King's presence, even though Henry was hunting and he had to meet him in a tent in a park. Though there was none of the splendid ceremony of Court, the King determined to make the Bishop feel as uncomfortable as possible by not taking any notice of him. He told his courtiers not to say anything either, so when Hugh came in and greeted the King there was no answer, and no one spoke.

Taking no notice of this, Hugh went up to the seat next to the King and sat down on it. Henry still took no notice. He had hurt his finger while he was hunting, and had on it a large leather finger-stall. It was slightly loose, so he asked for a needle and thread and started to sew it tighter. Still no one spoke. Henry was waiting for the Bishop to say he was sorry, and he thought the longer he kept quiet the more uneasy the Bishop would become. He would make Hugh realize that he was a great king who must be obeyed.

But Hugh was thinking of something else. His sense of fun was getting the better of him. Henry II might be a great king, but he was descended from a poor tanner who lived at Falaise, in France. And now, watching the King sewing his leather finger-stall, he could be quiet no longer.

"You remind me of your relatives at Falaise," he said.

There was a horrified silence. The courtiers were sure that the King would get up and strike Hugh for this insult. But, instead of that, Henry looked at Hugh and suddenly started to laugh. He laughed and laughed, till the courtiers thought it wise to join in, and then he took Hugh aside and forgave him.

Hugh gave him a little talk on the duties of kings in keeping their subjects under control, and Henry ended by allowing him to deal with the Forester, who was the cause of all the trouble, as he thought best.

When Henry died, and his son Richard the Lionheart came to the throne, Hugh still guarded the rights of the Church against Richard's attempts to get the Church's money for his wars.

"Do you not know that this King loves money as a parched and thirsty man loves water?" some one asked him.

"He may do," answered Hugh, "but I will not be the water for him to swallow."

And again, when Richard died and his brother John became King, Hugh continued to see that he kept within the bounds of what was right.

Hugh's great work, and the one by which he is still remembered, was the building of the beautiful cathedral of Lincoln. It was here that he was buried when at last he died, worn out with his struggles on behalf of the Church against three Kings, all of whom, however, had looked on him as a friend. King John was at his funeral, and the King of Scotland; and the nobles and princes of the land carried his bier up the steep hill to the cathedral he had built, to honour the gay, simple man who had never wished to leave his cell in the forest, but who from duty had become one of the great statesmen of England.

XXXII

ST FRANCIS OF ASSISI

(ST FRANCIS'S DAY: OCTOBER 4)

TWO years after St Hugh died a local war was being fought in Italy between the great town of Perugia and the town of Assisi, which the Perugians wanted to make their own. In the course of it a gay and wealthy young man of Assisi named Francis was taken prisoner, and, for a year, kept in captivity, in Perugia. All the time he was in prison he was longing to be free again to lead the life of pleasure to which he had become accustomed; but when at last he was set at liberty and went back to his home he found that he was discontented with all the things that he had thought he wanted. So he made preparations to go to war again, this time against the Germans, who were invading Italy.

The night before his departure he dreamt that he was in a great hall, hung with splendid armour, all marked, as the Crusaders' armour was, with a cross.

"These," said a voice, "are for you and your soldiers."

Francis became more excited than ever, and, as he set off, he told his friends and his family: "I know I shall be a great Prince."

But he had not gone very far before he had another dream in which the same voice asked him: "Which is better—to serve the servant or to serve the Lord?"

"Of course, to serve the Lord."

"Then why do you make the servant your master?"

Francis, realizing what this meant, left the expedition and went back to Assisi, determined to serve God, the Lord of all, in any way he could. He found that he was seeing the people of his town with new eyes. Instead of the great, wealthy families who had been his friends, he noticed for the first time those who were living in terrible poverty and disease. The beggars and lepers, he realized, were not people to be passed by without looking at them, but God's children for whom Jesus Christ had died. For the love of Jesus he determined to spend the rest of his life dedicated to 'the Lady Poverty.'

He gave away all his money and possessions, even his

As he was praying he saw an angel flying towards him

clothes. He served the sick and the poor. And gradually he collected round him a number of other people whom he called the Friars Minor—the 'little brothers'—who, with him, would love people for Christ's sake, and remind them of His life and teachings.

At first there were very few of them. They lived together not far from Assisi where, round the little Chapel of St Mary of the Angels (or the Porziuncula, as it came to be called) which the Benedictines had given them, they built huts of wattle, straw, and mud. But soon so many joined them that the Friars Minor were able to make their way all over Europe, and even to the East, to try to convert the Mohammedans.

Above all things Francis was always teaching that Christians must show themselves Christians by their love for one another, as Jesus had told them. His favourite festival was Christmas and it was he who was the first to have a Crib, with its 'Bambino,' in churches, to make people realize the great story of how 'Love came down at Christmas.' He even tried to persuade the Emperor to make a special law that men should provide well for birds and beasts as well as for the poor, so that every one should have a reason for rejoicing.

The animals and the birds were his friends—he called them his brothers and sisters—as well as the lovely things of nature. He composed a poem called *The Canticle of the Sun*, in which he praised God for Brother Sun and Sister Moon and Sister Water, so helpful and humble and pure, and Brother Fire

Through whom Thou givest light in the darkness
And he is bright and pleasant and humble and strong

and for all God's gifts, even Death.

Then, in the year 1224, almost on the very day that the first Friars Minor landed in England, God showed that He was pleased with Francis. Francis had gone with three companions far up on a mountain called Alverna, to spend forty days in prayer and fasting. As he was praying he saw an angel flying towards him with outspread wings. In the centre of this vision appeared a cross. When it vanished Francis found that in his own hands and feet and side there had been printed the five wounds of Christ Himself. His longing to become like his Master had been answered.

XXXIII

ST DOMINIC

(ST DOMINIC'S DAY: AUGUST 4)

DOMINIC was born at Calaruega, in Old Castile, in 1170, the year that St Thomas Becket was murdered in England. His father and mother, Felix and Joanna de Guzman, belonged to the nobility of the country and were well known to the King, Alfonso IX. Until he was fourteen Dominic was educated by his uncle who was a priest at a town not far from Calaruega, and even when he was a boy he was quite sure that he himself wanted to be a priest. So, at the age of fourteen, his parents sent him to study theology at the University of Palencia.

Here he not only studied the ideas of religion but tried to put them into practice. One day he sold all his books and gave the money to the poorest people in Palencia. Among them he found a woman who was crying bitterly. When he asked her what the matter was, she told him that her only brother had been carried away into captivity by the Moors and that she now had no one in the world to look after her or earn a living for her. As Dominic had given away all his money he could not ransom her brother, so instead he offered to go himself and become a slave to the Moors in her brother's place. Though she would not allow him to do this, he tried once more to sell himself into slavery so that the money could be given to the poor.

But the great men of the Church had other plans for the young priest. With his goodness, his learning, his gift of speaking, and his noble birth, he became one of the well-known people of the time. Dominic is one of the few saints of the Middle Ages whose physical appearance we know of, for we have a description of him by one of his followers: "In height he was of the middle size; his features were regular and handsome; he had a fair complexion, with a slight colour in his cheeks; his hair was reddish and he kept his beard close shaven. His eyes were blue, brilliant and penetrating. He had a powerful voice, pleasant to listen to."

When King Alfonso sent the Bishop of Osma on a mission to France to arrange a marriage for his son, Prince Ferdinand, Dominic was chosen to go with the Bishop. They had to pass, of course, through the southern part of France—Toulouse—and here they found that most of the country had fallen away from the Christian faith. Men and women were following the teaching of the Albigenses, who took their name from the town of Albi. The Albigenses preached that Jesus was not God but only a very good man; they said it was wrong to marry and have families and that the sooner the human race died out the better, for they believed that the body was an evil thing which would not, as Jesus taught, rise again at the Last Day. This teaching made Dominic so surprised and angry that he spent the whole night arguing with the people with whom he was staying. They were Albigenses, but like all the heretics said that they were the only real Christians. The result was that in the morning his host and his family announced in public that they saw how wrong they had been, and were received back into the Church.

Dominic and the Bishop, whose name was Diego d'Azevedo, went on their way and were at last successful in arranging the marriage between Prince Ferdinand and the daughter of a French count. They returned to King Alfonso with the news and were sent back again with a splendid retinue, to fetch the Prince's bride back to Spain. They arrived to find that she had died suddenly in the meantime, and as they reached her father's castle, they were met by her funeral procession. This was such a shock to Dominic and Diego, the Bishop, that they determined to devote the rest of their lives to becoming missionaries and preaching the Gospel to the heathen. So they sent the cavalcade back to Spain and themselves went to Rome to see the Pope. Diego wanted to get permission to resign his bishopric and, with Dominic, to go off to far lands as a simple missionary.

The Pope, however, would not allow it. He said that the real danger to the Christian faith at that moment was nearer home. It came from the Albigenses, whose teaching was spreading all over the south of Europe like wildfire, among the wealthy and the powerful as well as among the ordinary people. So Dominic and Diego went back to Toulouse to help the Cistercians—the Order of monks founded by St Bernard of Clairvaux—whom the Pope had appointed to try to make the Albigenses see their mistake and come back to the Church.

The Cistercians were not successful, and very soon Dominic went back to Rome again to tell the Pope why he thought this was. One reason was that too many of the clergy had become wealthy and were living worldly lives, while the leaders of the Albigenses were living as poor men, trying in that respect to imitate Jesus and His disciples. Another reason was that neither the Cistercians nor the ordinary parish priests were preaching or trying to answer the arguments of the Albigenses, as Dominic had answered them on that first night when he had stayed among them. So Dominic suggested that he should be allowed to form a new Order in the Church— an Order of Preachers. Those who belonged to it should be learned in the Christian faith and be able to explain it to other people as well as to answer attacks on it. And they should live in poverty and simplicity like

125

the followers of St Francis of Assisi, who just at that time in Italy had gathered round him a body of 'Friars Minor,' and was showing people a new way to live the Christian life.

At first the Pope refused. He said that there was no need for a new Order. But one night he had a dream. In his dream he saw the Church tottering and beginning to fall, when suddenly two men rushed to it and held it up—they were Francis of Assisi and Dominic. So the Pope granted Dominic's request and gave permission for him to found his Order of Preachers to go and work among the heretics. Dominic went into the great Church of St Peter in Rome to give thanks to God for this decision, and while he was there he saw a vision of St Peter and St Paul who told him that God had chosen him to go and preach the Gospel in this way.

Soon Dominic's new Order, which became known as the Black Friars because of the colour of the robes worn by its members, spread all over Europe. Somebody made a pun of their name, Dominicans—*Domini Canes*, which is Latin for 'Dogs of God'—and often in paintings of St Dominic you will see a dog at his side, carrying a lighted torch, as a reminder how, by their learning and their preaching and their poverty, St Dominic's Order of Preachers—the 'Dogs of God'—went out to carry the light of the Gospel in Christian countries which had become dark with heresy.

Another thing you will find in pictures of St Dominic is a rosary. A string of beads to keep count of the number of prayers said was something that had been used hundreds of years earlier by the Christian hermits who lived in the desert. Dominic made a new arrangement of these beads, so that the prayer said on most of them was the Angel's greeting to Mary, when he told her that she had been chosen to be the Mother of Jesus: "Hail, Mary, full of grace, the Lord is with thee: blessed art thou among women and blessed is the fruit of thy womb, Jesus.''

This was the very thing that the Albigensians did not believe. Because they thought the body was evil, they denied that God had taken human flesh from the Virgin Mary. But one day when Dominic was praying very earnestly Mary herself appeared to him and told him

Dominic's new Order became known as the Black Friars

that by using the Rosary and saying this prayer many Albigenses would be brought back to the truth. So, among the simple people of the south, Dominic taught the devotion of the Rosary and found that this did more good than all his arguments and sermons. And when at last there was a crusade of the Christians against the heretics, Dominic himself, all through the battle of Muret, knelt before the altar of a little church not far from the battlefield saying the Rosary. It had seemed impossible that the Christians could win, for the odds against them were so great. But they did. And their commander, Simon de Montfort (the father of the Simon de Montfort we read about in our English history books), believed that the victory was a miracle due to Dominic's prayers.

XXXIV

ST ANTONY OF PADUA

(ST ANTONY OF PADUA'S DAY: JUNE 13)

THIS saint, who is known in history by the name of the Italian city where he spent his last years, was born in 1195 near Lisbon, in Portugal, and given the name of Ferdinand. His father, Martin de Bouillon, claimed to be a descendant of the Godfrey de Bouillon who was the hero of the First Crusade, and had a post at the Court of King Alfonso of Portugal. Ferdinand was sent to the cathedral school in Lisbon, and when he was only fifteen entered a monastery there. As the subject of which he was most fond was the study of the Bible, he soon asked if he might be allowed to go to the branch of the monastery at Coimbra, a little way to the north of the city, where there was a famous school devoted to scriptural studies. For eight years he worked very hard, and by the time he was made a priest he knew as much about Holy Scripture as anyone in Europe.

One day there called at the monastery five Franciscan friars who were on their way to Morocco to found a mission there. As Ferdinand talked to them he became more and more interested in these followers of St Francis of Assisi (who at that time was preaching in Italy). A year or two later, when the bodies of those five Franciscans, who had been martyred by the Moors, were brought back to Coimbra to be buried there, Ferdinand decided that he would leave his monastery, become a Friar and go to Morocco to carry on their missionary work.

He went to the Friary at Olivares, not far from Coimbra, where he was made a Franciscan and took a new name, Antony. Then he set off for Morocco. A severe illness caused him to start back to Portugal in the spring of 1221, but his ship was caught in a violent storm and driven on to the coasts of Sicily. With the rest of the crew and passengers he got ashore at Messina, where he went straight to the Franciscans in that town. They told him that, in the following month, all Franciscans were going to meet at Assisi and that St Francis himself would be there. So, with the rest Antony set out to that famous gathering where over 3000 Franciscans met. Afterwards he was sent to a small friary in the mountains where, as a priest, he could say Mass for the lay-brothers.

He had been there about nine months when an ordination was held at his Friary and the special preacher for the occasion failed to arrive. After several Dominicans attending the ceremony had refused to preach because they had not prepared a sermon, the Father Provincial signalled to Antony to come forward and give an address. As Antony had taken the vow of obedience, he could not refuse—and the subject he chose to talk about was 'Obedience.' He preached so well that when he had finished it was decided that he must leave the Friary and become a preacher, visiting all the districts round about. Soon his preaching drew such crowds that St Francis himself sent a message that Antony was to be appointed preacher for the whole of Italy.

The fame of Antony's preaching soon spread, until even the market-places of the towns were not large enough to hold all who wanted to listen to him, and a platform had to be carried out to a field or hillside to provide room for all the people—sometimes as many as forty thousand—who would come in from the country-side round about to hear him.

Antony did not always stay in Italy, for across the border in France the Albigenses were just as strong as they had been ten years before, when St Dominic was preaching to them. So Antony turned his steps, as Dominic had, to Toulouse, and it was while he was there, in the capital of the heretics, that one of the many miracles which occurred in his lifetime happened. An Albigensian named Bonvillo was arguing with Antony that Jesus was not really present in the Blessed Sacrament and demanded that a sign should be given. He said he would keep his mule without any food for three days and

The fame of Antony's preaching soon spread

would then bring the animal a bundle of oats. At the same time Antony should bring the Blessed Sacrament in procession from the church. The two could then judge—by the mule's conduct—how real the presence of Jesus was. Antony protested that this was no test of faith at all and that such a thing ought not to be done; but the crowd shouted him down and insisted on it. Antony spent the three days in continuous prayer, and when the test was made, though Bonvillo pushed the oats right under the nose of his ravenously hungry mule, the animal took no notice of them until Antony, bearing the Blessed Sacrament, had left the market-place and returned to the church.

In pictures of St Antony—and especially in paintings of him in Franciscan churches—you will often find this story of Bonvillo's mule represented; just as in all statues of St Antony (and there is one in nearly every Catholic church, for he is a very popular saint) you will see a reference to another story told about him. One day when he was reading his Bible and thinking in what way he could best preach the truth of Jesus, Jesus Himself appeared to him as a Child. So St Antony is usually shown holding the Child Jesus in his arms and standing on an open Bible.

Antony died when he was only thirty-six, worn out with his labours and journeys in preaching the Gospel, and was buried in Padua in a great, new church which the people of the city built in his honour.

XXXV

ST ELIZABETH OF HUNGARY

(ST ELIZABETH'S DAY: NOVEMBER 19)

ST ELIZABETH of Hungary, or, as she is sometimes called, St Elizabeth of Thuringia, is still known to the Germans as their 'dear St Elizabeth,' and is one of the best loved of all their saints. She was the daughter of one of the kings of Hungary, but when she was only four the powerful ruler of Thuringia asked her father if she might be brought up at his court, which at that time was one of the most brilliant in Europe, and, when she grew up, marry his son. So, when she was just a child, Elizabeth went to live in splendour in the great castle of the Wartburg among the poets and the 'Minne-singers' whom the King liked to have round him. The Prince whom one day she was to marry, whose name was Ludwig, was a boy of nine, and from the very first moment they met the children became the dearest of friends.

They were married when Elizabeth was fifteen and Ludwig twenty, in the year that the old ruler died and Ludwig became King in his place.

During her girlhood Elizabeth was so devoted to religion that she was sometimes laughed at by the more worldly people at court. One day there was a great service in the Church of St Catherine at Eisenach which was always attended by the royal family in much pomp. During this Princess Elizabeth suddenly left her place and put the crown she was wearing at the foot of the great crucifix. Her mother-in-law, who was shocked by this breach of etiquette, whispered to her that this was not the time or the place to do such a thing, and ordered her to put the crown on again. But Elizabeth, in tears, answered: "Dear lady mother, please do not scold me. Here I see Jesus, Who died for me, wearing His crown of thorns. How can I wear in His presence this crown of gold and gems? *My* crown seems a mockery of *His!*"

When Elizabeth herself became Queen her husband was called away to attend the Emperor on a journey to Italy, and that year terrible storms and floods, causing famine and plague, burst on Thuringia. Though she was only nineteen, Elizabeth insisted on taking charge of everything personally. Each day a certain quantity of bread was baked in the palace, and she herself served it out to the poor who came to the gates of the Wartburg, giving them all their just share. In this way, by what to-day we should call 'rationing,' she managed to see that no one actually starved, and when the autumn came she sent the people into the harvest fields with scythes and sickles, and to every man she gave a shirt and a pair of new shoes.

To deal with those who were sick she had a special hospital built below the Wartburg, in which there were twenty-eight beds. She herself visited it daily to attend to the needs of the patients. In order to have money for them, and for the alms she distributed throughout the whole of Ludwig's territory, she sold her jewels and her beautiful clothes, and even some of the State robes. This made some of the selfish courtiers very angry, but when Ludwig came home again he said she had been quite right, and he confirmed everything she had done in his absence.

But he soon had to leave her again—this time to go on a Crusade. But before he got as far as the Holy Land he caught a fever and died. As he was dying he commanded his knights and counts who stood round his bed that they should carry his body to his native land and defend his Elizabeth and their children—with their life-blood, if necessary—from all wrong and oppression. When the news arrived at the Wartburg Elizabeth cried: "Now all the world and its joys are dead to me!" and fainted from grief.

Ludwig's brother, Henry, decided that he would now become ruler of Thuringia instead of Herman, the little son of Ludwig and Elizabeth; and in the depth of winter she and her children were forced to leave the Wartburg.

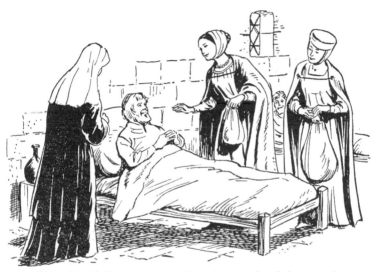

She visited daily to attend to the needs of the people

Henry forbade anyone in the neighbourhood to take her in, because he was afraid it might lead to a revolt against him; but at last she found some kind people in an inn who allowed her to stay there, and for some weeks she supported herself and her children by spinning wool.

But before long the knights and counts got back to Thuringia with Ludwig's body, and they remembered their vow to their dead king. They forced Henry to be content with the title of Regent: they put young Herman on the throne as King; and they saw to it that Elizabeth was given the city of Marburg as her own property. Elizabeth's own relatives suggested that, as she was still only twenty, she should marry again. But this she refused absolutely. She had loved only Ludwig as long as she could remember anything, and no one, she swore, should be allowed to take his place.

At that time St Francis of Assisi had just founded his new Order of poor preachers, living a life of charity and poverty; and it was to them that Elizabeth turned. She wished to join them and herself become a beggar; but her confessor forbade her to, although he said she might become a member of the Third Order of St Francis, which was meant for those who still lived ordinary lives in the world. So she built a great Franciscan hospital at Marburg, and devoted herself entirely to the care of the sick for the few years of life that were left her. She died when she was only twenty-four.

They buried her in the church attached to her hospital, and after her death so many miracles were worked there that it became a place of pilgrimage in Europe, almost as famous as the shrine of St James at Compostela in Spain. And within four years of the death of 'the greatest woman of the Middle Ages,' as she has been called, a great church at Marburg was built and dedicated to St Elizabeth.

XXXVI

ST WILLEBOLD

(ST WILLEBOLD'S DAY: NOVEMBER 2)

ON the feast of All Souls in the year 1230 a young man of twenty-two came to the little village of Berkheim, on the road between Memmingen and Biberach, in the far south of Germany. Nobody took very much notice of him. He was dressed like a pilgrim,

They were sure the hay must have caught fire

and his clothes had become ragged in his journeys. The landlord of the Crown Inn, seeing that he looked worn and ill, told him that he could spend the night in the hay-loft, for the inn was so full that there were no beds free. The young man, who gave his name as Willebold, grate-fully accepted the landlord's offer, and dragged himself up to the loft, where he threw himself down, tired out, on the sweet-scented hay and clover.

Suddenly at midnight—so the story says—the church bell began to ring, and the villagers, wondering what it could be, hastily dressed and went out into the street. They thought it must be a fire warning, and when they looked at the inn and saw a light coming from the hayloft they were sure that the hay must have caught fire and rushed up with buckets of water ready to put it out. But all they found was the young pilgrim lying dead, with a strange, unearthly light playing round his body.

They did not know who he was, but next day they took up the body reverently, and the parish priest buried it in the cemetery of the village church. Not very long afterwards miracles took place at the tomb, and the story of the unknown young pilgrim was told in towns far from Berkheim. Among those who heard it were Willebold's parents, though they did not at first realize that the boy was their son.

His real name was Albert von Calw, whose father was a nobleman of the house of Beutelsbach. The year before Albert had left the family castle and gone alone on a pilgrimage to the Holy Land, taking the name of Willebold. They had had no news of him since he left, but they were expecting his return; and he was, in fact, making his way home when he had died from sickness and exhaustion in the hay-loft at Berkheim.

The villagers, of course, thought that his father would want to take the body back to be buried in the family chapel; but, instead, Albert's parents put up a memorial to him in the church at Berkheim, where he had made his last pilgrimage from earth to heaven, and on it they had carved this sentence: "Here rests Willebold, who lived so that he is now an associate of the saints." And even to-day crowds still visit the shrine.

XXXVII

ST LOUIS IX

(ST LOUIS'S DAY: AUGUST 25)

WHEN St Willebold went on his pilgrimage to Palestine the Mohammedans, who hated the Christians, had conquered much of the Holy Land and were ill-treating the pilgrims who went to Jerusalem to see the places connected with the life and death and resurrection of Jesus. So the Christian kings and princes were called together to make a war for the Cross—a crusade—to win back Jerusalem for the Christians. On one of these crusades—the third—had gone our Richard the Lion Heart, King of England; but that Crusade was not really successful, nor were those which followed it. Yet for another fifty years these wars went on, fought always to try to recapture the Holy Land from the Mohammedans, but sometimes joined by people who merely wanted adventure and an excuse for fighting and seeing the world.

The Seventh Crusade, which was led by King Louis IX of France, set out in 1248, though the King had actually "taken the Cross"—as the vow to go on a crusade was called—four years earlier when he was very ill. Most of his courtiers did not want him to go and, even more, did not want to go themselves. Louis's mother and his wife and his friends all begged him to leave the fighting to others, and to stay at home and govern his kingdom. Even the Bishop of Paris tried to get him to give up the idea.

"You were very ill, sire, when you took the Cross. You did not really know what you were doing."

"That is what you really think? I was very ill and did not know what I was doing?"

"Yes, sire."

"Then," said the King, "I will tear it from my shoulder." And he pulled off the red cross which had been sewn on the shoulder of his cloak to show all men that he had taken a vow to go on a crusade, and gave it to the Bishop.

Every one was pleased. The King asked: "I am not ill or out of my senses now, am I?"

"No, sire," said the Bishop.

"Then," said the King, "give me back my cross, for I will neither eat nor drink until it is on my shoulder again."

The Bishop and the courtiers saw that the King was so in earnest about the matter that it was useless to argue with him any more; but they thought that if none of them took the Cross he would still not be able to set out.

Then on Christmas morning the King managed to change their minds. It was the custom for him to give them a new suit of clothes, and he asked that they would all meet him, in these suits, at the Dawn Mass of Christmas. There in the church they found that on the shoulder of each of the cloaks was sewn the red cross of the Crusaders. The King had ordered it to be done secretly during the night, and none of them in the morning dared take them off.

So at last the Crusade set out. Louis determined, instead of sailing direct to Palestine, to try first to conquer Egypt, where the enemy would not be expecting him. At the beginning he had a good deal of success; but at last food began to grow scarce, and there was sickness in the army, and there was nothing for it but to turn back home. Louis himself fell ill, and the army stopped at a little village in the desert where suddenly they were surprised and surrounded by a Mohammedan army.

There was terrible slaughter. The Mohammedans, pitiless and merciless, killed all the sick and wounded and all the ordinary soldiers. The knights were offered their lives if they would pay ransom or turn Mohammedan. If they were too poor to do the one or too brave to do the other they too were killed. Louis himself was taken prisoner and threatened with death.

But nothing would shake him.

"You have but to say one short sentence, 'There is one God, Allah, and Mohammed is his Prophet,' and you

He refused to become Mohammedan

shall go free and in honour," said the Mohammedan leader.

"Never."

"Many of your knights have been offered this."

"And their answer?"

"Their blood is now staining the desert sand."

"They gave their lives," said Louis, "rather than deny the Faith of Christ. Do you expect me, their king, to do less? I am your prisoner. Do with me what you will."

But the Mohammedan leader had no intention of killing the French King. He knew that the people of

France would pay any sum he asked to ransom Louis, just as, fifty years before, the people of England had paid a ransom for Richard the Lion Heart. And Louis agreed to the ransom so that he could go once more to France to raise another army for the Cross.

For sixteen years he stayed at home, and so well did he rule his people, keep the peace, and see that justice was done to all, that the country had never been happier. But in his heart he never forgot his vow to return and free Jerusalem from the infidel, and in the end, though he was tired and ill, he set out for the east once more. This time he sailed to Tunis, but he could go no further. He was too weak even to move, and a month later he was dead.

As his lips moved for the last time the courtiers standing round heard him whisper, "Jerusalem! Jerusalem!"

XXXVIII

ST ALBERT THE GREAT

(ST ALBERT'S DAY: NOVEMBER 15)

AMONG the many German knights and counts who went with the Emperor to Italy on that journey when St Elizabeth's husband, Ludwig, had to leave her for the first time was a very remarkable boy of about fifteen, named Albert. He was the eldest son of the Count of Bollstedt, and he was travelling to Italy in the care of his uncle, who was in the Emperor's service, in order to study at the University of Padua.

What made Albert remarkable was his interest in everything. Of all boys who have ever lived he looked most closely at what he saw. He wanted to know the 'how' and 'why' of things; and his observation was so exact that, for instance, his description of an apple from the rind to the core has never been bettered. When, as a young boy, he was learning to hunt in the woods and heaths round the family castle he would even notice and remember the behaviour of wild falcons and wonder why some trees grew taller than others. When there were various kinds of fish for dinner he would examine them in detail before he started to eat them. He was the first person really to notice insects—no one studied them till four hundred years later—and the first to classify flowers as wing-shaped, bell-shaped, and star-shaped. The deer and the squirrels in the forest, the cattle in the fields, and the fish in the river, the spider spinning its web in a corner —all the ordinary things that most of us just notice casually Albert would look at so carefully that he was able to give descriptions that have not been improved upon even by modern scientists with all the instruments they can now use.

He was equally interested in why things happen. When he was still in his 'teens at Padua he was watching some workmen cutting up blocks of marble and discussing with them why certain sculptures on them seemed out of proportion. Another day, he pushed to the front of a crowd which was watching the opening of a well and waiting anxiously to see whether a man who had been made unconscious by the vaporous gas would recover, though two of his companions had died.

When Albert grew up he wrote thirty-eight books dealing with every department of human knowledge. That was seven hundred years ago, but many of his observations on climate and botany and geography and physics might, says one of his biographers, "have been taken from a modern text-book," and in 1941 he was proclaimed the Patron Saint of all scientists.

But it was not, of course, Albert's learning that made him a saint. The reason he was interested in all natural things was because he saw in them a reflection of the wisdom of God, Who had made them. He had a passion for exact truth, because he was sure that all truth, of whatever nature, must lead to God, Who is Truth; and he was always very careful to distinguish between what he had actually seen for himself and what other people had told him.

Before he left Italy he joined the Dominicans, and later he was sent by them to teach at the Universities of Cologne and Paris. Here his most famous pupil, whose brilliance he recognized and encouraged, was St Thomas Aquinas. In 1260 Albert became the head of the Dominicans in Germany and, because he was ordered to, allowed himself to be made Bishop of Ratisbon. But he resigned two years later, and retired to Cologne to spend the rest of his life teaching and writing.

St Albert had a special prayer "against temptations."
He prayed "not to be led astray by false words about
nobility, religiosity, and excessive searching after knowledge." He was himself a noble and could, if he had
wished, have been one of the great rulers in Germany.
He was a 'religious' and a bishop, and he knew how many
people tried to look pious when they were really nothing

He saw in them a reflection of the wisdom of God

of the kind (that is what 'religiosity' means). One of his
sayings was: "It is better to give an egg for the love of
God when you are alive than to leave money for a
cathedral full of gold when you are dead and do not
need it." And, above all, this great scientist knew that
there is such a thing as 'excessive' searching after knowledge—the kind of idle curiosity that just wants to know
things for the sake of knowing them, or even for pride
in discovering them, and not because that knowledge
leads to God Who created everything.

XXXIX

ST THOMAS AQUINAS

(ST THOMAS'S DAY: MARCH 7)

THOMAS, the youngest son of Count Landulf of Aquino, was born in his father's castle among the mountains in the year 1226. His family was related to the Emperor himself, and it was expected that Thomas would become, like his elder brothers, a knight and a soldier. For his early education he was sent to the Benedictines at Monte Cassino, not very far away from his home; but he was so clever that when he was ten his masters found they could teach him no more, and he was sent to the University of Naples. While he was there he decided that he wanted to join the Dominicans—that Order in the Church which, you will remember, St Dominic had founded chiefly to study and to preach to the people, so that they should be able to understand the truths of the Christian religion. As a Dominican friar he went to Rome to continue his studies, and he was still so brilliant that his superiors sent him next to Cologne to study under the most learned man in Europe, St Albert the Great.

But he took some time to get to Cologne, because his brothers, who thought it a disgrace to have a friar in the family, kidnapped him and took him back to the family castle and locked him up there for two years, trying to get him to change his mind. In the end his sisters helped him to escape by letting him down the castle walls in a basket. Some other Dominican friars were waiting for him, and at last he got to Cologne. There he listened to the teaching of Albert the Great so carefully and said so little himself that he was nicknamed "the dumb ox"—he was very fat, and had a big, calm face, and *looked* rather like an ox—but when St Albert heard of it he said, "Do not make any mistake; his voice will be heard throughout the world."

And so it has been. For Thomas Aquinas had perhaps the greatest brain that any man in Europe has ever had, and he used it in writing a long book all about the mean-

His sisters helped him to escape

ing of the Christian religion, which is still used as the correct and official teaching of the Church. When he was a little boy there was one question he had asked over and over again—"What is God?"—and he spent his life answering it and helping other people to answer it.

Wherever he was his brain was always working, thinking out the answers to the clever heretics. Once he was at the court of King Louis IX of France—St Louis the Crusader—and suddenly at dinner, quite forgetting where he was, he brought his great fist crashing on the table so

147

that the goblets shook, and said aloud, "*That* will settle the heretics!" And the King, because he was a saint, did not think this was bad manners, as the other courtiers did, but immediately sent his secretary down to the seat where Thomas was sitting, telling him to take down the friar's argument, in case he should forget it.

Because Thomas was so wise, he was the most humble of men. One day when it was his turn to read to his brother friars during their meal the Superior suggested that he had mispronounced a word. Thomas immediately re-read it with the Superior's pronunciation. Afterwards some of the friars said to Thomas that he should not have done it, since Thomas's pronunciation was right and the Superior's wrong.

"No," said Thomas. "The pronunciation of a word is of little importance, but humility and obedience are of the greatest."

Thomas knew that not every one could follow the learned arguments of scholars, and that most Christians were simple people. But he saw, too, that the simplest person can understand what Jesus said at the Last Supper when He took the bread, saying, "This is My Body," and that this meant that, wherever the bread of Holy Communion was consecrated, there was Jesus Himself. So Thomas composed a series of great hymns about the Blessed Sacrament, which are still known by their Latin names, *Pange, lingua,* and *Tantum ergo* and *O salutaris* and *Adoro Te,* and are still sung every day all over the world.

XL

BLESSED RAMON LULL

(BLESSED RAMON'S DAY: JULY 3)

WHEN James the Conqueror, King of Catalonia and Aragon, led a fleet against the Moors and captured the island of Mallorca from them, one of the knights in his service was named Lull. After the conquest Lull decided to stay in the newly-won island, where the King granted him much land, and in Palma, the capital, his only son Ramon (Raymund) was born about the year 1232. Ramon was brought up to be a courtier, and when he was fourteen he became a page at Court and the companion of the King's two sons, Peter and James. He was about ten years older than Prince James and became his tutor, travelling all over Spain and to other parts of Europe until, one day in 1256, the King announced that he intended to make Prince James in due course King of Mallorca. So, as Ramon was a Mallorcan by birth, he was sent back to his native island in charge of the future King. Back in his home, he settled down, married and had two children; but he continued his gay courtier's life with his friend and pupil, the Prince.

One of Ramon's hobbies, at which he was particularly good, was to make up gay songs and the music to them. On a summer evening in 1263 he was working hard on one of these songs—first scribbling the words, then humming the tune. Somehow he could not get it to go as he wanted it; and the whole of his mind was set on it when he raised his head and gazed into space, trying to get the tune in his head to come the right way. Suddenly he thought that some one was looking at him. He turned his head, and there on the wall he saw "our Lord God

149

Jesus Christ hanging upon the Cross" and looking at him with "great agony and sorrow." Trembling with fear, he stopped writing and ran from the room to escape from that piercing look. In the morning he decided it must have been some kind of dream, and, being a practical young man, put it out of his mind and went on with his song. But no sooner had he started than the figure of Jesus Christ appeared again. And so it happened three more times until Ramon gave in and realized that it must be God's will that he should leave worldly things and "devote himself wholly to His service." From that moment he decided that he must become a missionary and give the whole of his life to preaching the Gospel until God should allow him to give his life as a martyr for Jesus.

But to whom should he go? Living when and where he did, it was obvious that he should preach to the Moors. He saw, too, that as he had the gift of writing, he ought to devote that gift to writing books to show the Mohammedans that their beliefs were wrong. So the first thing he did was to learn Arabic. As there were many Moors still living in Palma, it was not difficult to find teachers and to practise conversation. For nine years he studied, till his Arabic was so perfect that he could write as easily in that language as he could in his own, and he knew so much of Arabic thought and religion that he was able to lecture on it in the greatest centre of learning in Europe at that time—the University of Paris.

He wrote books, too, in his own language, Catalonian, and in Latin—about 300 altogether during his long life. The most famous of them was a kind of religious novel called *Blanquerna*, which is still one of the great books of European literature and which was a model three centuries later for *Utopia* by Sir Thomas More, the British Saint.

At first at Palma Ramon still lived with his family in

his great house, but one day he heard a sermon about St Francis of Assisi (who had died about six years before Ramon was born) and how he had given up everything to follow Jesus in complete poverty. He decided that he would work with the 'Friars Minor' and, after having set aside all the money needed for his wife and children to live their ordinary lives, he gave away all the rest of his possessions and went to his friend, Prince James—who

He ran from the room to escape that piercing look

had now become King of Mallorca—to ask if he might have some land for a missionary college where he could train twelve Franciscans for work among the Moors. James himself founded this college at Miramar, and here Ramon began in earnest to prepare for the next stage of his life's work.

There were many obstacles in his way and he was nearly sixty before the Pope at last gave his permission for Ramon himself to go to Africa. And then a strange thing happened. Ramon was at Genoa in Italy; he had taken his passage, and all his luggage was on board a boat for Africa, when what he calls "a great temptation" overtook him. He suddenly realized that even if he went to Africa the Moors would never allow him to preach and argue with them. They would surely either immediately kill him or imprison him. Would it not be better if he stayed in Europe and did a little more of his writing and teaching before he went to death? Also he was very ill. So he let the boat go without him. No sooner had it sailed than he became so much worse that the doctors thought he was dying, though they could not find any cause for his illness. But Ramon realized that, after all, he had been a coward and, sick as he was, he made his way to the harbour and boarded the next boat for Tunis, urging the sailors to put to sea at once lest anything should stop their departure. Once he was afloat his illness left him, and by the time they reached Tunis he was as well as he had ever been in his life.

When he arrived in the Mohammedan city he started preaching in the Arabic he spoke like a native and said that, if anyone could show him that Mohammedanism was right, he would become a Moor and give up his Christian faith. This, of course, meant that all the learned Moors of the city started to argue with him, but he answered them so well, quoting all their own books against them, that they were all "astonished and confounded," and he was arrested and taken before the Caliph. On the advice of the majority of his council the Caliph condemned him to death, but the sentence was changed to one of banishment.

In Europe once more, he continued his writings and again visited Paris to argue with those who, though Christians, had allowed some of the ideas of a great Mohammedan teacher to influence their work. He also visited his home in Mallorca. But in his heart he was certain that he must go back to Africa, in spite of his banishment and the danger of almost certain death if he returned. At the age of seventy-five—an old man with a long white beard—he made the journey across the Mediterranean for the second time, and faced a furious mob in an African market-place where he cried out: "The law of the Christians is holy and true and the sect of the Moors is false and wrong and this I am prepared to prove." This time he was put into prison, but even in prison he continued to convert learned Moors who came to talk to him, and at last the King of the country ordered that he should be expelled from the land on pain of death if he dared ever to return.

And, of course, Ramon did return—when he was eighty-three. His friend, King James, wrote to the King of Tunis asking that Ramon might be allowed to teach in safety: "King, we inform you that our subject, Ramon Lull, is in your city of Tunis where he wishes to live and stay. Therefore, O King, since we know well the said Ramon and are sure that he is a good, learned man of upright life, we pray you that it may be your will and pleasure, for our honour, to look favourably on the said Ramon; and for this we shall be grateful to you."

So, for a little time, Ramon was able to carry on his work in peace. But not even the King of Tunis was able to prevent the mobs from attacking the Christian teacher. One day, when he was preaching about Jesus, there gathered round him a crowd more fierce than any of those from which in earlier days he had escaped; and, before anyone could interfere, they had stoned him to death.

XLI

ST ELIZABETH THE PEACEMAKER

(ST ELIZABETH'S DAY: JULY 8)

ELIZABETH, who was born in Saragossa in 1271, was the niece of Blessed Ramon Lull's friend, King James—that is, the daughter of his elder brother, Peter. She was the favourite grandchild of King James the Conqueror, who called her his 'little angel of God' and always kept her by his side at Court till his death when she was six years old. She was only twelve when she was married to Denis, the eighteen-year-old King of Portugal. The marriage was, of course, like nearly every royal marriage in those days, a matter of state. It was a way of obtaining the friendship of the young King for Elizabeth's father, the King of Aragon. But though King Denis did not love his girl-bride and Elizabeth had not wanted ever to marry but to become a nun, she determined that she must do her duty by obeying her father and by doing all she could for her husband and his people when she became Queen of Portugal.

King Denis wanted to make Portugal a contented and happy country, and to accomplish this he set men to work on the land so that there should always be enough wheat for the people's bread. He actually became a farmer himself—he is sometimes known in history as 'Denis the Labourer'—and Elizabeth tried to help his plans by giving money to build a great college at Coimbra where young orphan girls were trained in farming so that they would be good wives for farmers' sons.

But the King did not always approve of the Queen's generosity in other ways, for Elizabeth looked after as many poor people as she was able, and sometimes he thought that this alms-giving was a waste of money which could be used for other purposes. There is a story told that one winter day, when she was carrying in her lap a lot of gold which she meant to distribute among those who needed food and warmth, she met the King. She expected him, as usual, to find fault with her; but this time he said nothing—for all that he saw in her lap was a handful of roses.

Whether or not this tale is true (and it is the kind of story that people who remembered her kindness might make up afterwards, for the same incident is told of her great-aunt, St Elizabeth of Hungary), there is another story which is certainly historical. There was a particular page whom the Queen usually employed to go on her errands of charity. One of the King's courtiers, who hated the Queen, told the King that she was fonder of this page than she was of him. King Denis believed the wicked courtier and determined to get rid of the page, so he gave orders to a lime-burner to throw into his lime-kiln the first person who should bring a royal message to him. Then he called the Queen's page and sent him with a message to the lime-burner.

The page, suspecting nothing, started out—but before he reached the lime-kiln he heard a bell from the church ringing for Mass. He turned aside into the church, heard Mass, and stayed for some time afterwards saying his prayers before he continued on his way with the King's message. Meanwhile the King had grown impatient and sent the courtier who had first told him about the page to see what had happened. As this courtier was the first person to bring a royal message, the lime-burner seized him and threw him into the kiln. When shortly afterwards the page arrived the lime-burner said to him: "When you return to the King, tell him I obeyed his command."

"What command?" asked the page.

"The King will understand," said the lime-burner. "Just give him that message."

When the King heard it and realized what had happened, he thought it was God's way of telling him how wrong he had been to believe the wicked courtier. And from that moment he tried to be kinder and to show more love to the Queen.

Denis and Elizabeth had a son and a daughter; but as the son, Prince Alfonso, grew up he grew less and less fond of his father who, he thought, was not fair to him and showed more favour to other people. When the Prince was about twenty-nine years old, he and his father actually went to war against each other and a battle between them was fought at Coimbra. As neither gained the victory, the Queen was able to reconcile them for a time; but a year and a half later—it was in the year 1323—they started fighting again and met on the battlefield of Alvalade. The two armies were already engaged: stones and arrows were thick in the air and the knights were just preparing to charge to support their infantry. Suddenly into the battle galloped the Queen on a mule. She was alone, because no one else had dared to follow her. Both armies looked at her as if she had been a vision from Heaven, and the fighting stopped. The King and the Prince were both in tears at this proof of Elizabeth's courage and of her love for them. There on the battlefield they became friends once more. The Prince knelt and kissed his father's hand; the King gave his son his blessing; and Elizabeth the Queen was given the name by which she is still known—'the Peacemaker.'

Not very long afterwards King Denis died and two days after his death, Elizabeth, who had fulfilled her duty as his wife for forty-three years, became at last what she had wanted to be since she was twelve—a nun. She spent the last eleven years of her life as a 'Poor Clare,' as

the women of the Franciscan Order were called, at
Coimbra. When she was dying, her daughter-in-law,
Beatrice, was by her bedside when suddenly Elizabeth
said: "My child, bring a chair for this Lady." But
Beatrice could see no one else in the room and asked:
"Which lady, Mother?"

The Prince knelt and kissed his father's hand

"The Lady in white clothes who has just come in,"
said Elizabeth, raising herself to welcome the visitor.

But still Beatrice could see no one. She only heard
Elizabeth say:

> "Mary, Mother of Grace,
> Mother most merciful,
> Protect us from the foe
> And take us in the hour of our death."

And, having said this, she smiled and fell back, dead.

XLII

ST CATHERINE OF SIENA

(ST CATHERINE'S DAY: APRIL 30)

THE city of Siena is built at the top of a tall hill, and at the two highest points are the cathedral and a convent dedicated to St Dominic. Between them is a deep valley in which is a great well whose waters were famous all over Italy. Not far from this fountain lived in the year 1347, a dyer named Giacomo Benincasa, the youngest of whose many children was a girl named Catherine. One evening when she was about six years old she and her brother Stephen stopped to rest on the steep hill leading up to St Dominic's, and as Catherine was looking up at its tall tower it seemed to her that the sky suddenly opened and she saw Jesus sitting on a throne in Heaven, with St Peter and St Paul and St John standing beside Him. But her brother Stephen saw nothing, and he could not understand why his sister stood so still looking up into the sky. He shook her arm. She turned to him, and when she turned her eyes back again to the sky the vision had gone. She threw herself on the ground and started to cry bitterly.

From that moment she determined that she would give the whole of her life to Jesus and to no one else; and when the time came for her to marry she refused the man her father had chosen for her. Instead she asked to become a nun in the Dominican convent. But her parents would not allow this, and when Catherine still refused to marry anyone they grew angry at her disobedience. They sent away the servant and made Catherine do all the work. Her brothers and sisters made fun of her. But Catherine bore it all without complaining, for she thought, The saints and the martyrs had to bear far worse things than this. Then one day her father found her kneeling in her room, with a white dove nestling on her shoulder. He remembered that the Holy Spirit often came in the form of a dove, and he thought that perhaps he was wrong and that it was God's will that Catherine should live as a nun, keeping herself only for Jesus, as she wished.

She went about Siena helping the sick and poor

So Catherine became a member of the Third Order of St Dominic, which meant that she did not actually live in the convent but stayed at home, observing the Rule. For three years she lived in her room in absolute silence, going out only to her Communions and prayers in the great convent church on the hill-top. At the end of this time she came out of her 'desert' and went about Siena helping the sick and poor.

All the city came to love her. There was a young

nobleman who had been condemned to death for a very small offence. He was very bitter about the injustice as well as being very afraid to die. Catherine went to visit him, and immediately he became calm and brave. He asked only one thing. "Stay with me!" he said to Catherine. "Then I shall be all right. I shall die content."

"Be comforted, my brother," said Catherine; "I shall be waiting for you at the place of execution."

She kept her promise. At the place of execution she was not only waiting, but she stood near him, and, as she put it in one of her letters, "I bent over him and held him as he lowered his head, reminding him of the blood of Jesus."

At the time when Catherine lived the Popes had been driven out of Rome and were living in France at Avignon. They were bad times for Italy, and Catherine was quite sure that one of the reasons was the absence of the Pope. When the people of Florence, who had made the Pope very angry, asked her to go to him at Avignon and make their peace with him she set out to do so. And she did more than that. She persuaded the Pope to come back to Rome, where the Head of the Church ought to have been. After that not only the Pope but kings and rulers of republics and leaders of armies asked her advice, and she was kept so busy that several young noblemen became her secretaries and wrote the letters she dictated to them. No woman, except St Joan of Arc, did so much to alter the history of Europe as St Catherine of Siena.

But to her, of course, these things were just one of the ways she showed her love for Jesus; and the greatest day of her life was when, praying in a church before a crucifix, she found that He had given her the greatest proof of His love for her, and that on her hands and her feet and in her side were the marks of the wounds of the Crucified.

XLIII

ST JOHN NEPOMUCENE

(ST JOHN NEPOMUCENE'S DAY: MAY 16)

IN a village called Nepomuk, in Bohemia, about the year 1340 a boy by the name of John Wölflein was born. He was not very strong and could not work on his father's farm; but he loved to read and study, so his parents decided that he should become a scholar, and when he was older they sent him to the University of Prague. When he was about thirty he became a priest, and was so good and clever that the Archbishop appointed him to very important posts, and at last the Queen herself chose him to be her confessor. She gave him charge, too, of all the money she distributed to the poor, and as the royal almoner, as the post was called, John of Nepomuk became a well-known person at court.

On the throne of Bohemia at that time was Wenceslaus IV, as different a man from his saintly ancestor, 'good King Wenceslaus,' as could be imagined. His nickname was 'the Drunkard'—and sometimes 'the Lazy'—and every one was very sorry for his wife, whom he ill-treated. But John was able to strengthen her by keeping her firm in the Christian Faith. His prayers and his advice became precious to her, because they helped her to bear patiently the sad life she had to lead. But the more trust she showed in her confessor the more the King hated him.

One day, in one of his drunken fits, Wenceslaus sent for John and ordered him to tell him what sins the Queen had mentioned in her confession. John reminded him that no priest, in any circumstances whatever, is allowed to say one word of what is told him in confession, and that the King, in asking him to 'break the seal of confession,' was guilty of sacrilege as well as treachery to his wife. The sterner John was in his refusal, the more determined the King became to make him speak. He threatened him, he bribed him with promises of money and power, and, as John still refused, he at last ordered him to be thrown into a dungeon where he kept him for several days without food.

At the end of this he again had him brought before him and again questioned him; but still John told him nothing, and, in a terrible rage, Wenceslaus ordered him to be tortured. But this time, in front of all the courtiers, who were wondering what was going to happen, the Queen threw herself on her knees before the King and, at last, by her entreaties and her tears gained John's release. His close imprisonment and torture had made him very ill, and he had to be carefully nursed; but as soon as he was better he came back to court again, preaching and teaching as if nothing had happened. But in his heart he knew that the King would never forgive him, and in order to prepare the Queen for what he was certain would happen he took as the text for his first sermon after his return the words: "Yet a little while and ye shall not see me."

He was right. A few days later, as he was returning to the palace from distributing the Queen's charitable gifts to the poor, the King, who was standing at a window, noticed him and was again seized with one of his mad fits of drunken anger. He ordered his guards to go down immediately into the street and arrest John. For the last time, when the priest was brought before him, the King ordered him to reveal the secrets of the confessional; but this time John did not even trouble to answer him. The King made a sign to the guards who then bound John tightly hand and foot and carried him out into the street to the bridge over the river Moldau. Then they threw him over the parapet and watched him drown in the deep waters.

From the palace window King Wenceslaus too watched. He saw the body sink, and was happy that the priest was at last dead. But, just as he was turning away, he noticed that the body had come up again,

The more determined the King became to make him speak

and that above it was a light which seemed to be made of five stars hovering over the place where the guards had thrown John in the river. The King rushed out of his palace like a madman, and rode away to one of his fortresses far away from Prague, where he stayed, refusing to see anyone, for many weeks. But the Queen had the body of her saintly confessor buried in great state.

St John of Nepomuk thus became a martyr for the seal of confession, and, in pictures and statues, he is

163

always represented as having his finger on his lip and five stars round his head. And, on the bridge over the Moldau, a metal plate with stars on it still marks the place where the bad King Wenceslaus had him thrown to his death.

XLIV

ST BERNARDINE OF SIENA

(ST BERNARDINE'S DAY: MAY 20)

IN nearly all the towns and cities of Italy in the
fifteenth century there were feuds and fighting.
Sometimes the quarrels were between the servants of
two rival houses, like that between the Montagues and
the Capulets which Shakespeare shows in his play *Romeo
and Juliet*; but more often it was between the two great
parties, called the Guelphs and the Ghibellines, who were
trying to get power over the whole country. There was
no peace anywhere, for no one could be sure that on any
day a fight might not start over something or other and
innocent people get killed.

Bernadine, who was born near Siena in the same year
St Catherine died there, decided it was his duty to preach
"Peace." He was a nobleman's son who had become a
Franciscan friar, and when he was thirty-seven he
started to travel all over Italy on foot, trying to bring
the people to a better way of life. He was one of the
greatest preachers there has even been. Sometimes he
would talk to the crowds for four hours at a time and the
crowds were so large—in Milan there were thirty thousand people listening to one of his sermons—that only
the great market-place would hold them.

While he was preaching he used to hold in front of him
a board in the middle of which was painted the letters
I.H.S. These stood for the Latin words *Jesus Hominum
Salvator*, which mean, 'Jesus, the Saviour of Men' and
which are a reminder of the Holy Name. Round the
letters were painted golden rays. When the sermon was
over Bernadine would ask the people to show that Jesus

was their real Lord and that His Name was the one they should honour most. They were Christians, and that was more important than being Montagues or Capulets, or Guelphs or Ghibellines. And if they were all true to the Holy Name of Jesus they would have to stop their feuds and fights for their earthly lords.

Everywhere he went Bernardine managed to persuade men to take down from the walls of palaces and churches and houses the coats-of-arms of the rivals and put in their place the letters I.H.S., so that they would always be where every one could see them and would remind the citizens to be loyal to the Prince of Peace.

But, of course, not every one wanted peace, and it was not long before those who wanted the fights to go on tried to stop Bernardine. They complained to the Pope that he was really teaching the people idolatry and getting men to worship a piece of wood with some letters painted on it. So the Pope sent for Bernardine and forbade him to preach any more or to show his tablet with the 'sacred monogram'—as the I.H.S. is called—until his teaching had been examined by a council of learned scholars and bishops. Bernardine immediately obeyed. When the matter came to trial before the Pope Bernardine was shown to be so right that the Pope invited him to come and preach in Rome and offered to make him Bishop of Siena.

Bernardine, however, refused to accept the bishopric. He preferred to remain a poor friar, tramping the roads of Italy, and preaching the gospel of peace. One of the causes of much of the evil and misery he saw about him was, he thought, that the people were very poor and when they had not enough money to buy food and clothing they borrowed it from men who made them pay almost double for the loan. So all the time they grew poorer and more miserable. In his sermons Bernardine was always attacking the moneylenders as the most wicked of men, but he saw that they took little notice of him and that he must try to do something practical to alter things. So everywhere he could he started groups of Christian people who were willing to lend money to very poor people when it was really necessary, without charging them any interest. This charity was to be done for the sake of Jesus, and the societies were called Monte-di-Pietà, which means 'Charity Bank.' The sign chosen for them was a little green hill made up of three mounds, and on the middle one either a Cross with Jesus on it or a flag with a picture of the dead Christ.

In pictures of the saints you can always recognize St Bernardine, because he will be holding either the board with the I.H.S. or a little Monte-di-Pietà, with its three mounds. The great work he did in bringing peace and helping the poor in the name of Jesus made him known as the 'Apostle of Italy.'

The 'Apostle of Italy'

XLV

ST JOAN OF ARC

(st joan's day: may 30)

JACQUES D'ARC—or, as we should call him in English, James of Arc—was a farmer in the little village of Domremy. He had five children, of whom the youngest was named Joan. When she was a small girl she used to help to look after her father's sheep, and as she got older she learnt to sew and spin for the family; but, like St Geneviève long before her, she would often go away alone to think about God and to say her prayers. And, just as happened with St Geneviève, God sent angels and messengers to talk to her.

She was thirteen when she first heard her "voices," as she called them. She was in her father's garden when there was a great light beside her, and out of the light spoke a voice which she thought was the Archangel Michael. St Michael, she knew, was the leader of the warrior-angels, for she had heard often the passage from the Bible which tells how St Michael was God's champion in the war against Satan.

And it was not surprising that the warrior-angel should have been chosen to give a message about the terrible war which was going on in France at the time. For nearly a hundred years, there had been war between the English and the French. The English kings had said that they ought to be kings of France too, and had come with armies to try to conquer France. No one in France could live in safety, because soldiers went about the countryside robbing and destroying. There was no law. Even Paris was in the hands of the enemy, and the true King of France, Charles, had not been able to be crowned.

The message which St Michael gave to Joan was that God had seen "the great misery of France" and had chosen her to put an end to it. The *last* part was so surprising that Joan could hardly believe it, and for four years she said nothing about it to anyone. But during those four years the voices still came to her, and other saints besides St Michael appeared to her; while in the country the war got worse and worse. Charles, the Dauphin—for until he had been anointed with the holy oil at his coronation he could not be called King—was preparing to leave the country. The English were besieging Orléans, and when it was taken they would be masters of France. All hope would have gone.

So, when she was seventeen—it was the beginning of the year 1429—Joan knew she must wait no longer. She must obey the voices that God had sent her, even though what they ordered her to do was something no girl had ever done before. St Geneviève had lived through times when France was overrun by foreign armies, and she too had been chosen to save her people. But she had done it by becoming a nun and offering her prayers and by helping and encouraging people when they were afraid. But Joan was told to act quite differently and in a way that every one would say was mad. She, who had barely been out of her village, was to go and find the Dauphin and have him crowned. She, who was a simple peasant girl, was to dress herself in a man's clothes and lead an army to drive the English out of France.

"I am only a poor girl," she said to her voices. "I do not know how to ride and fight."

"It is God who commands it," they answered.

So she set out, and though the officer to whom she first went to ask him to take her to the Dauphin said, "Take her home to her father and give her a good whipping," she persevered until at last she got to the Court at Chinon.

169

Here too they thought she was mad and played a trick on her. The Dauphin told one of the courtiers to dress up in the royal clothes while he himself pretended to be one of the courtiers. But Joan, though she had never seen him before, came straight up to him and told him why she had come. When he still hesitated she whispered to him a secret which the voices had told her—something which no one in the world except himself knew. That made him change his mind and, though many of his courtiers still tried to prevent it, he let Joan have her way.

Dressed in a suit of armour, mounted on a white horse, and bearing a white banner with the words "Jesus: Mary" on it, she rode at the head of the French army to Orléans, which was surrounded by English troops. She ordered the attack and drove the enemy away from the city. There were other battles, which she won; and at last she was able to take the Dauphin safely to Reims, where in the great cathedral he was anointed and crowned King. Then she went back to fighting the English.

The English troops did not think she was mad. They thought she was a witch who had got her strange power from Satan, and when in a battle her enemies managed to capture her they brought her to trial for witchcraft.

Her enemies shut her up in a dungeon; they kept her chained to a great log of wood; they did not allow her to receive Holy Communion; and they questioned her again and again to try to make her say that her voices did not really come from God. The ungrateful King made no attempt to rescue her; even some priests and bishops tried to make her believe she had done wrong and that her voices were either her imagination or evil spirits; and in the end they burnt her at the stake in Rouen.

But Joan, though she was only nineteen, was as brave

and as certain before her judges as she had been on the
battlefield. Whatever she did, she knew she must be
faithful to God. And when an English soldier, who had

She went into battle

tied together two sticks in the form of a cross so that she
might have it to hold as she was dying, said, "God have
pity on us, for we have burnt a saint," he was telling the
truth.

XLVI

ST JEROME EMILIANI

(ST JEROME'S DAY: JULY 20)

JEROME EMILIANI was born in Venice in 1481. His father died while he was still a boy, and when he was fifteen he decided to become a soldier in the army that Venice was raising against attack by the other nations of Europe. The Republic of Venice, which included much land round the city itself, had many towns that other nations wanted, and the French and the Spanish and the Germans were joining together in a league against it. So Jerome, like so many other Venetians, felt it was his duty to get ready to defend it when the time came. And once he became a soldier he found that he enjoyed the life very much, and for eleven years he had a wild time and did many evil things for which afterwards he was very sorry.

In the year 1508 he was sent in command of a company of soldiers to defend the fortress of Castelnuovo, not far from Treviso, against the attacking Germans. He found the castle in a bad state. The walls were crumbling away, and he did not see how he could hold it against the enemy. Although he and his men fought very bravely, they were easily overcome, and he found himself imprisoned in a deep dungeon, with fetters on his wrists, and his leg chained to a huge and heavy ball of stone.

As the days went by he had time to think of the bad things he had done in his life, and he grew more and more sorry for them. He started to say his prayers again, and he made a vow that if ever he got out of prison the first thing he would do would be to make a pilgrimage to a chapel at Treviso which was dedicated to the Blessed Virgin Mary.

No sooner had he made this promise to Our Lady than he noticed on the floor a small key. He did not remember having seen it before, and managed to pick it up. It was the key that unlocked his fetters. But, although he now had the key, he was chained so carefully that he still found it impossible to get altogether free. Then the same kind of miracle happened as had happened not long after

Jerome realized that some one was helping him to shake off all his chains

the days when Jesus had lived on earth and St Peter had been released from prison by an angel. Jerome realized that some one—he thought it might be Our Lady herself —was standing by his side, helping him to shake off all his chains and leading him out of his prison, opening all the doors before him as they went.

As soon as he was safe in the countryside he went, as he had promised, straight to the chapel at Treviso and told every one what had happened; and shortly afterwards, when the war was over and he was made Keeper of Castelnuovo, the first thing he did was to send the fetters and chains and the great stone ball to the chapel at Treviso to hang from the roof, so that all men would be reminded of the miracle.

He did not stay long at Castelnuovo, because his nephews in Venice needed him there to look after their education, and he himself wished to become a priest. In Venice he realized how many orphans there were who had no one to look after them and take an interest in their lives, and after a great plague and famine which swept over the land in the year 1528 there seemed to be more helpless and unfortunate boys and girls without a home than ever. So, with one or two friends, he took a house near the Church of St Rose and turned it into a home for homeless children.

Gradually other people came to help him, and he founded a new Order, whose chief work was to look after orphans and the poor and the sick everywhere. The headquarters of this society was in a tiny village called Somascha, not far from the city of Milan, and so the Order became known as the Somaschans.

Jerome himself never stopped doing good works, and it was while he was nursing people who had an infectious disease that he caught it and died. But in Venice people always remembered the Saint, who became the 'Knight of Our Lady' when the orphans to whom he and his followers had given a home dressed themselves in white in her honour and went through the streets and squares of Venice singing her hymns.

XLVII

ST THOMAS MORE

(ST THOMAS MORE'S DAY: JULY 9)

WHILE, in Italy, St Jerome Emiliani was fighting in the wars, there had come to the throne of England King Henry VIII. Henry VIII, like Henry II, had made one of his friends, called Thomas, the Chancellor, and hoped he would always do as the King wanted. His name was Thomas More. Besides being a very clever lawyer, he wrote books, and was a gay and amusing man, and the King liked to go down to Chelsea and visit him at his house there.

On one of these visits the King and Thomas walked chatting in the garden for more than an hour, and they seemed such good friends that afterwards More's son-in-law, William Roper, said to him, "You are indeed a fortunate man. The King had his arm round your shoulder as if you were his dearest friend."

"You are right, son Roper," said More, who knew that Henry really cared for no one but himself, "I think the King is as friendly to me as he is to any man in England. But that is nothing to be proud of, for I am sure that, if by having my head cut off he could win a castle in France, my head would go."

About this time the King got tired of his wife and wanted to get rid of her and marry some one else. When the Pope told him that he could not do such a wicked thing, he decided that he would pay no attention to the Pope, but would get his own bishops to do what he wanted in England. So he had himself proclaimed Head of the Church in England, and made people take an oath that he and not the Pope was the person who could say what it was right to do. If they would not do this he had them put in prison and then killed.

A great many people in the Church saw no harm in this, but others said that no one but the successor of St Peter—the Pope—could be called Head of the Church, and they were ready to die rather than take the oath. Everybody thought that Thomas More would take it. He was not a priest or a bishop. He had a happy family whom he loved very dearly, as they loved him—especially his daughter Margaret, who was married to William Roper—and they and his other friends would say that, when so many bishops were taking the oath, there could be nothing wrong in it for him. But he knew there was. He said that it was as impossible for the Church in England to make its own particular laws which the rest of the Church did not agree with as it would be for the City of London to make one of its rules an Act of Parliament which should be lawful for the whole country.

When the day came for him to appear for trial he was at home with his family. He had to go to Lambeth Palace, which was the opposite side of the river Thames from his house, and as he went down to the riverside to take a boat he would not allow them to come with him, as they usually did, to say good-bye to him there. He was afraid that, because he loved them so much and did not want to leave them, he would become weak and take the oath after all.

So he took with him only his son-in-law William Roper and four servants, and got in the boat to row across the river. He was sad and troubled, and still had not quite made up his mind what to say at Lambeth. Then, just before they got to the landing-steps, he whispered to Roper, "Son Roper, I thank our Lord the field is won."

He was sent to the Tower of London, brought out again for a public trial, and condemned to death. On his way back to the Tower for execution his daughter

Margaret suddenly broke through the guards who were taking him there, and the crowd standing round, and, "openly in the sight of them all," threw her arm round his neck and kissed him.

Five days afterwards he was beheaded on Tower Hill. As he was going to the scaffold a man who in the old days had found comfort and wisdom in the advice of Thomas

He was sad and troubled

called out, "Mr More, do you know me? I am as troubled as ever I was."

More answered, "I remember you very well. Go your way in peace and pray for me; and I will not fail to pray for you."

More made a very short speech to the people who had come to see him die. There was much that he could have said, but the King had sent a message asking him to say little, and Thomas More, like Thomas of Canterbury, Hugh of Lincoln, and all the statesmen-saints, always obeyed the King in things that the King had a right to ask. He ended his short speech by saying, "I die the King's faithful servant, but God's first."

They set up his head on a pole over London Bridge, so that all people should see that even a great man who was the King's friend was shown no mercy when he refused to put the King's wishes before everything else. But one morning the head was not there. In the night his daughter Margaret, with trusty friends to help her, had stolen it to keep it safe and hidden until she herself died, when it was buried with her—the relic of her beloved father who was also a saint.

XLVIII

ST IGNATIUS LOYOLA

(ST IGNATIUS'S DAY: JULY 31)

IGNATIUS was a soldier. He was born in 1491 in his father's castle of Loyola in Northern Spain, became a page at the Court of King Ferdinand and, as he grew older, a soldier-courtier, seeking worldly glory like a knight-errant of earlier days. In the year 1521, as an officer in the garrison of Pamplona which the French were besieging, he was urging the Spaniards not to surrender when he was wounded in both his legs by a cannon-ball. He was taken back to his home at Loyola where the wounds slowly healed—but left one leg shorter than the other. Ignatius, who was very vain of his appearance, insisted that the wound was reopened and part of the bone sawn off, even though it meant most terrible pain. He bore it without flinching, but afterwards he became very ill and was for a long time unable to leave his bed. During this time he became very bored, as you would expect in one who had been used to a life of action and gaiety and danger, and he asked for books to read. "A romance, a story, anything to pass away the time!"

Among other books they brought him a life of Christ written by a Saxon monk and much to his surprise Ignatius found that this was the book he wanted to read again and again. Gradually Jesus and His life and death became so real to him that he determined that when he recovered he would give up the worldly career he could have had at Court, and become a soldier of Christ. And when at last he was well again he set off on a pilgrimage to the great shrine at Montserrat, and there, before the altar, hung up his sword and dagger to show that henceforth he was going to fight in a different kind of warfare. But before anything else, he must do penance for his many sins and try to find out how he could best serve his new Master. Not far from Montserrat was the town of Manresa and just outside it a cave, with its entrance almost hidden by briars and bushes. Here Ignatius went to live in solitude, like the hermits in the desert, for many weeks until he had overcome all the temptations of the Devil to turn away from God and please only himself once more. First of all, he thought of the meaning of life and of its purpose—to serve and praise God in this world so that one may be with Him always—and he thought how terrible sin is that it makes men turn away from their true purpose. Then he thought about the life of Jesus as it is told in the Gospels; and after that, about His suffering and death for our sakes. Lastly he thought about the joy of Heaven and the reward promised to the "good soldier of Jesus Christ."

On a stone in the cave at Manresa—which is still pointed out to you if you visit it—he started to write down this method of prayer; and later he made it into a little book, called *The Spiritual Exercises*, which for four hundred years has been used by hundreds of thousands of people who want to be better Christians 'for the greater glory of God.' "For the greater glory of God" (A.M.D.G., the first letters of the Latin words which mean: *Ad Majorem Dei Gloriam*) was Ignatius's motto.

When at last he came out of his cave at Manresa he seemed so different that a friend asked him: "Did you see devils and witches in there?"

"Much worse," said Ignatius. "I saw myself."

After a visit to the Holy Land, so that he might see and worship at the very places where Jesus lived and taught and suffered and rose again, Ignatius decided that he would study to become a priest. This meant for him who had once been proud, vain, noble and a soldier, to begin at the beginning and sit by the side of schoolboys learning Latin. Though many people, including some of the schoolboys, laughed at him, he did not mind. He was doing it 'for the greater glory of God.' He persevered with his lessons as he had persevered with everything else, and soon he was ready to go to the University of Paris to finish his training.

A cave with its entrance almost hidden

While he was at Paris, he met some other young men who gathered round him (the story of one of them, St Francis Xavier, is told later in this book) and on the Feast of the Assumption (August 15) 1534, seven of them met in a church at Montmartre. Ignatius told them of his plans. If they would join him, they should all take the vows of poverty, chastity, and obedience, and offer themselves for service in the Holy Land. But if, for any reason, it was impossible to work in Palestine, they should go to Rome and place themselves at the Pope's service as his special 'soldiers' to do whatever he ordered. They called themselves the 'Company of Jesus,' and by using the word 'company' they meant to show that they regarded themselves as part of an army under military discipline. This was the beginning of what is to-day the largest and most powerful of all the Orders in the Church: the 'Society of Jesus' (for the Latin word for 'company'— *societas*—was later translated as 'society'), the Jesuits.

It was the soldier in Ignatius which insisted on the perfect discipline which has always been one of the distinguishing marks of his 'Company.' When he himself was sixty, he said that the slightest sign from the Pope would send him aboard any ship to sail anywhere in the world. A nobleman who was standing near said: "But that would not be very prudent."

"Prudence, my lord," answered Ignatius, "is the virtue for those who command, not for those who obey."

As it happened, it was impossible for the 'Company' to go to the Holy Land as they had intended. Instead they were used by the Pope as missionaries in the fight against the new doctrines preached in Europe by Martin Luther, which was gradually spreading from Germany to England and France. As three centuries earlier Dominic had insisted on good learning, as well as good lives, as a weapon against the Albigenses, and Ramon Lull had trained himself and others in Arabic to be able to argue with the Mohammedans, so now Ignatius made one of the objects of his 'Company' to give the best education possible to the young so that they would be able to defend the Faith at home as well as understand the languages and customs of the heathen abroad.

Ignatius saw another danger and did his best to guard against it. In the Church there were, unfortunately, too many men who were not worthy of their calling and who looked on it as a career, wanting only wealth and power and high places. So Ignatius laid it down that no member of the 'Company' was ever to accept a bishopric or other high post in the Church, except at the direct command of the Pope. But even in Ignatius's lifetime, the 'Company' as it grew larger produced so many brilliant men—they became almost the 'brains' of the Church—that Catholic kings and rulers started appealing to the Pope to give them high positions.

Ignatius became alarmed and himself appealed to the Pope.

"This," he said, "is a danger to the spirit of the 'Company.' The other Orders of the Church are like squadrons of cuirassiers, whose duty is to stand fast in their appointed places and face the enemy. It is right to bestow honours on them. But the Company of Jesus is like a troop of light horsemen always ready to go in any direction in skirmishing order at a sign from the Vicar of Christ. It is not in their nature to be fixed in one place."

"I have never heard such a petition before," said the Pope. But he saw the common sense of what Ignatius said and did as he asked.

Ignatius lived to direct his Company for sixteen years and when he died in 1556 there were already about a thousand of his followers, scattered in ten different countries, looking to him as to their 'General.'

XLIX

ST JOHN OF GOD

(ST JOHN'S DAY: MARCH 8)

JOHN of God was born four years later than Ignatius Loyola and died six years before him and like Ignatius, he founded a new Order in the Church: the Hospitallers or, as they are sometimes called, the Brothers of Charity. But as far as we know these two Spanish saints never met each other and certainly two men could hardly have been more different.

John was born in 1495 at Montemoro Novo in Portugal. His parents were very poor, and when he was only eight years old, John ran away from home with a traveller who had stayed for some days with them, telling tales of the wonderful things he had seen in his journeys. But the little boy found himself left alone in a village near Oropesa on the other side of Spain, four hundred and fifty miles away from his home. There was no one he could turn to; it was impossible for him to get back to Montemoro, so he worked as a shepherd-boy for a farmer of the district. There John stayed till he was about twenty, serving the farmer so well that the man decided to let him marry his daughter and become a partner in the sheep-farm. But John still wanted adventure and once more he ran away—this time as a soldier of fortune in the Spanish army which was going to Hungary to fight the Turks. Until he was forty he was a trooper in various parts of Europe, enjoying the dangerous, cruel, care-free life and forgetting all about the religious duties which his mother had taught him as a small boy and which, in his days as a shepherd, he had still remembered a little.

While he was a soldier he often risked death in battle; but it was facing death in another way that brought a change in his life. After one battle he was left to guard a great heap of booty. When his turn to guard it was over and another soldier came to take his place, it was found that much of it had been stolen under his very nose. Of course everybody suspected him of partnering the thief and of getting his share of the loot; and, even if that were not true, he had certainly failed in his guard-duty. He was tried by court-martial and condemned—so one account says—to be hanged on the spot. The rope was actually round his neck when an important officer happened to pass by and, pitying him, ordered that he should be allowed to live, on condition that he immediately left the regiment.

So he returned to Spain, and at last decided to go back to his native village and his parents. When he got there he found they were both dead and he was told that his mother had been dead for many years. She had in fact died from grief shortly after he had run away from home, for he was her only child and she had loved him most dearly.

When John heard this, he was terribly sad and blamed himself for the deaths of his parents. He saw, too, that there were many other people to whom he had done wrong in his soldiering days and he determined to spend the rest of his life trying to make up a little for all the evil he had done.

His first idea was to go to Morocco and give his life in martyrdom as Ramon Lull had done, but he soon came to feel that to be chosen as a martyr was too great an honour to expect and after he had consulted a priest in Africa about it he came home to Spain. He landed at Gibraltar, where he spent what little money he had on a wheelbarrow and some religious books and pictures and statues. He trudged the roads of Spain, selling these to whoever he could, until he came to the city of Granada.

185

While on this journey, so the story goes, he found a small child by the roadside, barefoot and badly clothed, just as John himself had been when he had been deserted at Oropesa. Immediately he lifted the boy on his shoulders and carried him as far as his strength would let him. When they reached a drinking-fountain, John suggested to the boy that they should stop and rest a little. The boy climbed down from his shoulders and said, holding out to him a pomegranate (which is a *pomo-de-Granada*, a Granada apple): "John of God, in Granada you shall find your Cross." Then he disappeared and John did not see him again.

When John arrived in Granada, he set up a little shop by the city gates where he continued to sell books and pictures and statues, as he had done on the road. But he soon felt that this was not enough to do to serve Jesus and atone for his wicked life, so he went on a pilgrimage to Our Lady of Guadeloupe and there he was told in prayer his real life's work. When he returned to Granada, he rented another house and turned it into a home for all the outcasts of Granada. Tramps and cripples, homeless poor and prisoners just let out of gaol—John gathered them all together and looked after them. When he needed money, he went out into the streets to beg for it. Though he had hardly any education and was certainly not a doctor, he managed somehow to look after his strange 'family' as if he were doctor and nurse and priest all rolled into one. At last John's 'hospital' became so talked about in the city that the Bishop—who was also the Mayor—sent to find out who he was and why he was doing this in Granada. John told the Bishop of what the Child had said to him and of the curious name by which he had been called.

"Then," said the Bishop, "John of God shall always be your name." And he gave him help and money to carry on his work in a bigger way, with helpers and a larger 'hospital.' In this way the Order of Hospitallers was started.

One of the stories men loved to tell about John was how, when a fire broke out in his hospital, he forgot about

John gathered them all together and looked after them

the danger of the flames and insisted on going back again and again until all his 'family' were rescued. And it is this incident which is still remembered year by year in the prayer which is said on his feast-day, reminding us of the saint who, "burning with love of God, could walk unharmed through flames."

L

ST FRANCIS XAVIER

AMONG the students at the University of Paris when Ignatius Loyola was studying there was another Spaniard whose name was Francis Xavier. Francis was younger than Ignatius. Like Ignatius, he was a nobleman—he had been born in his father's castle at Xavier—but unlike Ignatius, who was dressed like a beggar, he took pride in his appearance. He was so learned that he was already a professor and he looked on the Church as a career in which he could win great prizes. In fact, Francis rather despised Ignatius and one day, when he had given a particularly successful lecture and was day-dreaming about the famous name he was going to make for himself in the world, he was annoyed to see the beggar-student standing in the shadow of a building watching him. He hurried by, but he heard Ignatius's whisper: "What does it profit a man if he gain the whole world and lose his own soul?"

The more Francis thought about this, the angrier he became; but somehow the words never left him. Whenever he was doing something at which he excelled, and was doing it so well that men said he was bound to become the head of a college, he seemed to hear that whisper. It haunted him and at last he went to Ignatius and asked him what he ought to do. It was then that Ignatius told him of his idea for his 'Company of Jesus,' and Francis became one of his first followers, one of the seven who took the vow in the little chapel in Montmartre on August 15, 1534.

Xavier stayed with Ignatius during the early days in

Rome until the Company of Jesus was properly formed and had received the Pope's blessing. Then the King of Portugal sent a request that four Jesuits should be sent to preach the gospel in India, where the Portuguese had already a colony at Goa. But it was possible to send only one and the one chosen by Ignatius—though he was very sad to let his best-loved disciple go—was Francis Xavier.

At Lisbon, where the ship was to start, the King made

He hurried by, but he heard Ignatius's whisper

a great fuss of Francis and loaded him with gifts—"so many presents," Francis wrote to Ignatius, "that I do not know how I could stand them if I was not almost certain that in India they may have to be paid for with no less than life."

But when the time came to set sail, Francis, true to the rules of the Company of Jesus, refused to travel in the state the King wanted to give him. All he asked was a wool rug to protect him from the cold at the Cape of Good Hope and some religious books.

"But you must have a servant," said the King's

messenger. "Your position demands it. You can't wash your own clothes and cook your own meals. You will lose your dignity."

"Sir," said Francis, "it is this fussing about the wrong kind of dignity which has done such great harm to the Church. I mean to wash my own clothes and watch over my own soup-pot and look after other people's as well; and by doing this I do not think I shall lose any authority."

And so began the first missionary journey of Francis Xavier, who was to become the greatest missionary the world has ever known. In the ten years of life left to him after he landed in Goa, he travelled over South India, visited Cochin and Ceylon, went to Malaya and several other East Indian islands, entered Japan, and finally died waiting for a boat that never came to take him to China, where no Christian had ever been.

When Francis and his companions first went to Japan (where they landed on August 15, 1549, fifteen years to the day after the taking of the vow in Paris), they spent the whole of the first year learning the language, and with the help of their interpreter translating into Japanese the chief articles of the Christian faith. Not until he had become completely sure of the language did Francis start to preach, and then he went to as many different parts of the country as he could. One who was with him kept an account of his journeys: "Neither the cold nor the snow nor the fear of unknown peoples hindered the Father. On the sea, the pirates were everywhere; going by land, our troubles increased. We carried all our luggage in two wallets. It consisted of a surplice, three or four shirts and an old blanket which we both used at night, for there are no beds in Japanese inns. We thought ourselves fortunate if they lent us a straw mat or a wooden pillow. Sometimes, owing to the deep snow, our legs swelled and we fell in those bitter mountain paths. Poor, badly clad strangers, we were received very badly in certain places, laughed at even by the children and sometimes stoned." But so well did Francis preach the Gospel and organize local churches that within forty years of his death there were 400,000 Christians in Japan where, before his coming, the name of Jesus was unknown.

Yet it was China, of which great land he had heard fabulous tales, that he most wished to enter. And in this matter all arrangements seemed fated to go wrong. "You may be very sure of one thing," he wrote, "the Devil will be very sorry to see the Company of Jesus enter China, judging by the obstacles he puts in my way every day." Francis managed to get a Portuguese ship to take him as far as the island of Sancian, so near the mainland of China that it seemed just a short trip across the bay. But while he was waiting for a vessel to take him there, he became very ill and, in a little hut which his friends quickly built, he died.

The Chinese boy whom he had converted and who was with him when he died wrote: "Every day and every hour of each day, the Blessed Father looked with great desire and anxious longing for the Chinese merchant who had promised to take him to Canton. But Our Lord ordered it otherwise, having determined to bestow upon him, at that time, the reward for all the great labours and sufferings he had endured for His love and service."

LI

ST TERESA OF AVILA

(ST TERESA'S DAY: OCTOBER 15)

TERESA, who was born at Avila in 1515, had her first adventure when she was seven. She was the third child of a large family, and her favourite among her nine brothers was Roderigo, four years older than herself. Roderigo and Teresa liked to play at being hermits in the garden, but one day they decided that they would change from make-believe to earnest. They would run away to Africa and there the Moors would martyr them! With a stock of dried raisins that they had hoarded as food for the beginning of their journey, they thought they could walk to the sea-coast, begging for alms on the way. But before they had gone very far they met their uncle, who very firmly took them home to their anxious parents. Roderigo explained that it was really Teresa's idea, because she wanted to see God and thought the best way was to become a martyr as quickly as she could.

When she was only thirteen her mother died and Teresa was sent to school with the nuns at Avila. But as she became ill, she returned to her father and was brought up at home. Then, when she was twenty, she decided that she ought herself to become a nun and when her father forbade it, she ran away again—this time in company with another brother, Antonio, who, when he had left her at the door of the Carmelite Convent, went on himself to the Dominicans. The Carmelite nuns, of course, explained to Teresa that it was wrong to cause her father such anxiety, and immediately let him know where she was. When he realized that his daughter was quite determined to serve God in the religious life, he did not oppose it any longer and gave her his blessing.

For many years Teresa remained in this convent, but gradually she became dissatisfied with it. She felt that life there was being made too easy and that what had been founded as a House in which women could serve God in poverty, prayer, and obedience had become a worldly place where they lived in comfort, doing very

For many years she remained in this convent

much what they liked, free from the responsibilities of home and family life. She decided that she must try to reform the Carmelites and bring them back to the early and strict rule of the Order. To do this it was necessary to found a new House.

Teresa found it very difficult to obtain permission to do this, but, as she had never been daunted by difficulties, she went on trying until she succeeded, and in 1562 the first House of the 'Primitive Rule' was founded in Avila. These nuns were known as 'Discalced' Carmelites. 'Discalced' means 'without shoes,' and that gives you an idea of what was in Teresa's mind when she insisted that it was no use to think you could serve God properly if you were worrying about being rich and comfortable. In the rooms of her new convent there hung on the walls not crucifixes but plain crosses. When she was asked the reason for this, she explained: "If you would serve His Majesty properly" (she always referred to God as 'His Majesty'), "you must put yourself on the Cross."

After the first foundation, Teresa was allowed to found other 'Discalced' houses, and before she died she had started seventeen others in various parts of Spain. Many people, even in the Church, did not like this and called her 'the roving nun.' But nothing could stop her serving 'His Majesty,' for in her prayers Jesus came so close to her that all worldly hindrances and unkindnesses seemed nothing. When you are older, you can read the many books she wrote, some of them the best books about prayer in the world, like *The Interior Castle*, and some of them about her adventures, like *The Foundations*, which tells the story of how she founded her Houses.

Teresa was one of the most sensible and matter-of-fact people you could ever meet, even among the saints. When a certain girl wanted to become a nun and Teresa was told she had great devotion to God and loved saying her prayers, Teresa said: "Even though our Lord gives this young girl devotion, yet, if she has no *sense* she will never come to have any and then, instead of being of use to her House, she will always be a burden." If anyone should ever complain of the hard life of Christians, Teresa would remind that person: "Those whom His Majesty loves, He treats as He treated His Son." She was always full of gay courage and often remarked, "God deliver me from gloomy-faced Saints"; but when a priest told her that she herself was being looked on as a saint, she answered: "Father, during my lifetime I have been told I was handsome, and I believed it; clever, and I thought it true; and that I was a Saint—but I always knew people were mistaken about *that*."

Yet, when you come to learn more about her—as I hope you will—I think you will agree that Teresa of Avila was one of the greatest of the saints.

A few years ago one of the English Houses of St Teresa's Order of the Carmelites, at Aylesford in Kent, which had been well known in the Middle Ages, was turned once again into a monastery, and thousands of pilgrims now go there every year. And all around you in the cities and towns of this country you will find members of other Orders which were founded by the Spanish Saints—the Jesuits of St Ignatius, and the Blackfriars of St Dominic, and the Brothers Hospitallers of St John of God. Yet in the centuries immediately after the Reformation their houses in England were destroyed, and many Catholics suffered martyrdom in trying to bring this country and Germany back to the Faith.

LII

ST PETER CANISIUS

(ST PETER CANISIUS'S DAY: APRIL 27)

JUST as St Boniface is known as 'the Apostle of
Germany,' so St Peter Canisius, who was born in
1521, is called 'the Second Apostle of Germany.' At
the time of his birth a German monk, Martin Luther,
had broken away from the Catholic Church, and by his
preaching had influenced many of the German princes to
follow him and join his new 'Lutheran,' or 'Protestant,'
Church. So, by the time that Peter Canisius had finished
his studies at the University and taken his degree of
Master of Arts at Cologne, great parts of Germany were
no longer Catholic.

This made Peter very sad, and when he heard that
there was in the neighbourhood a member of the new
Order of the Society of Jesus, which St Ignatius Loyola
had founded a few years earlier to fight for the Faith,
Peter set out to visit him. The result of this was that
Peter Canisius himself joined the Society of Jesus and
before long went to Rome to see St Ignatius himself.
Many of the Jesuits were going as missionaries to far-off
lands, but Peter thought—and later said—that to defend
the Faith at home was just as important as to convert the
Hindus, and he hoped that he would be allowed to go
back to work in Germany. Fortunately for him, at this
time the Duke of Bavaria, who had remained faithful to
the Church, was very worried about what was going to
happen to the University of Ingoldstadt and sent to St
Ignatius for help. In the struggle between the Catholics
and the Protestants the universities, as centres of learning,
were very important, and the Duke was anxious that

196

Ingoldstadt should be in the hands of a good and fearless scholar. So St Ignatius decided to send Peter Canisius, with two others, to teach there.

Before he left Rome Peter went to pray at the tombs of

He went to pray at the tombs of St Peter and St Paul

St Peter and St Paul, and he has left a record of what he felt as he was doing so:

> They gave me their blessing and strengthened me for my mission to Germany, and seemed to promise their assistance to me as to an apostle to Germany. From that day forth Germany occupied more and more of my anxious thoughts, and I longed to spend myself utterly in life and death for her salvation.

Peter Canisius was only twenty-eight when he took up his work at Ingoldstadt, and he lived till he was seventy-six, spending all his time, not only at Ingoldstadt but later at many other places all over Germany where he was sent to preach and teach, in defending the Faith in learning and argument, with his tongue and with his pen.

He realized that one of the most important things to be done was to see that people, young and old, knew the simple truths about the Catholic Faith; so he wrote a short catechism, in Latin and German, which before his death went into two hundred editions and was translated into twelve European languages. This short catechism was intended for children and was an extract from the great catechism he wrote for students at the universities, which contained 222 questions, 2000 quotations from the Bible, and 1200 from the Fathers of the Church among the answers. It was the model for all late catechisms, and even two hundred years later there were many places where the word 'Canisius's' was used instead of the word 'catechism.'

Peter was one of the kindest and gentlest of men. He preferred just to state the truth and not to argue about it. He never lost his temper. When he first arrived at Ingoldstadt he found that the head of the school and library there was a disagreeable man who was spending the University's money on Lutheran books. Peter, though he could have done so, did not order him to change his ways, but instead performed so many acts of kindness, and said so many prayers for him, that in a very short time the man was overcome with shame, burnt the books he had bought, and mended his ways. Even the Protestants loved this 'Second Apostle of Germany' whom one of them described as "a noble Jesuit whose character no blemish stains."

LIII

BLESSED EDMUND CAMPION

IN 1556, the year St Ignatius Loyola died, St Peter Canisius brought twelve Jesuits to Prague, the city of St Wenceslaus and St John Nepomucene, to form a teaching-centre there at the church of St Clement. The Clementium, as it was called, soon became famous, and to it, in 1574, was sent a thirty-four year old Englishman named Edmund Campion, to learn and to teach and to be trained as a member of the Society of Jesus.

Campion's father was a London bookseller, and Edmund had been educated as a Protestant at Christ's Hospital and at Oxford. While he was at the University Queen Elizabeth I had visited it, and had been so struck by his brilliance that she had promised him her special favour, and recommended him to her favourite, the Earl of Leicester. It seemed that a great and successful career lay before him, when suddenly he threw it all up, became a Catholic, left England to finish his education abroad, and, after a visit to Rome, joined the Society of Jesus.

When he had finished his teaching and training at Prague, and had been made a priest, he had one great wish—to return to his own country and help to bring it back to the Faith. He knew how badly priests were needed there to give the sacraments to those who had secretly remained faithful to the Catholic Church, in spite of the Queen's persecutions. The state of affairs in England in 1580 was very like what it had been in Spain a thousand years earlier, when St Hermengild chose to

199

die rather than to receive Holy Communion at the hands of one who was not a true priest. In some ways it was worse because Queen Elizabeth had not only made a law that every one had to attend the new Protestant Church of England which her father, Henry VIII, had founded, but also had enacted that any Catholic priest who celebrated Holy Communion was, if he were discovered, to be hanged, drawn, and quartered as a traitor.

So the Faith had to be practised secretly, and it was during those years that in many great houses men made those secret rooms called 'priests' holes,' where priests could hide from the pursuivants—as the police of that time were called—when they searched the house trying to find and arrest them.

Campion knew how dangerous it would be for him to come back to England where so many people knew him, and he did not expect to be able to escape for long. But from the day he landed, disguised as a jeweller, he managed to spend thirteen months preaching and teaching and helping people, before he was betrayed and arrested while hiding in a 'priest's hole.' I hope you will one day read the story of those months, with their adventures and daring and hairbreadth escapes, but it is too long to tell here.

After he was captured he was imprisoned in the Tower of London, and horribly tortured before he was hanged, drawn, and quartered at Tyburn. But he never lost his courage and his wit, and the learning which had once won him the favour of the Queen. And before he died he made a speech to those who had condemned him which is worth remembering and has been remembered. As he is the last of the English saints to appear in this book, I am going to quote part of it in which he looks back to some of our own saints you have read about— priests like St Aidan, bishops like St Thomas of Canterbury and St Hugh of Lincoln, kings like St Edward the Confessor.

When he was asked by his judges: "What can you say why you should not die?" Edmund Campion, speaking for all those who were suffering with him and had been condemned as 'traitors,' said: "It was not our own death that ever we feared. The only thing we have to say now is that, if our religion do make us traitors, we are worthy

He was arrested while hiding in a 'priest's hole'

to be condemned; but if not, we are, and have been, as true subjects as ever the Queen had. In condemning us you condemn your own ancestors—all the ancient priests, bishops, and kings—all that was once the glory of England, the island of saints and the most devoted child of the See of Peter. For what have we taught that they did not teach? To be condemned with these old lights—not of England only, but of the world—by their degenerate descendants, is both gladness and glory to us. God lives. Posterity will live."

Though to-day, four hundred years later, what Campion prophesied has come true, and Catholics can again openly worship God in England, the persecution was continued for hundreds of years so strictly that the Faith here seemed almost lost, and the story now goes to other countries where the Church was still in freedom.

LIV

ST CAMILLUS DE LELLIS

(ST CAMILLUS'S DAY: JULY 18)

CAMILLUS was born near Naples in 1550, the year in which, in Spain, St John of God died. He was the son of a wild father who cared only for fighting and gambling and was usually away at the wars. Camillus's mother died when he was twelve, and the boy was taken charge of by relatives. They could do little with him. He was lazy and disobedient; he had a violent temper and always wanted his own way; and out of school hours he spent all his time with bad companions. So his relatives were glad to be rid of him when at sixteen, a lanky figure, already over six foot, he went off to join his father in camp and become a soldier.

The chief thing his father taught him was to be an expert gambler, and the two of them, when they were not fighting for some captain or other (for they sold their services to anyone who would pay them), used to tramp about Italy, winning money from whoever was foolish enough to play cards with them. But before very long the father became ill and died, very sorry for the way he had lived, and Camillus, who had nursed him and was now left alone in the world, decided that he too must try to lead a different kind of life. He went off to find one of his uncles who was a Franciscan, hoping to be allowed to become a friar. But, as he had become lame from a wound in his ankle which would not heal, this was impossible. When that was better, they said, and he was fit for the hard life they led, he might come back.

So Camillus went to a hospital, and, as he had no money, he offered to pay for the treatment by becoming a

203

servant there. All went well until he taught the other servants to gamble. Then they started to quarrel and neglect their work, and those in charge of the hospital, when they discovered a pack of playing-cards hidden in Camillus's bed, sent him away there and then, with his ankle still unhealed and without any money in his pocket.

He went back to soldiering and his old life. For the next five years he fought, first by land and sea, for Venice against the Turks, then for Spain in North Africa, defending Tunis, and finally for a company of adventurers whom he asked to join, because every man in it was said to be a gambler. At last, at the age of twenty-five, he realized that, what with the wild life he had led and his bad foot, his days of soldiering were over. When the company was disbanded he returned to Naples, where he immediately gambled away all that he possessed— his gun, his sword, his powder-flasks, even his coat.

With nothing left but his shirt, he turned beggar. One day when he was standing outside a church asking for alms a man went up to him and told him that such a one as he, young and strong in spite of his lameness, should be working for his living, not standing there begging. Camillus said that he was a disbanded soldier and that no one would employ him. The man immediately offered him a job as a bricklayer on a new monastery which was being built. And Camillus, in spite of the laughter of his companion and of his own fear that after his exciting life he would never be able to endure the dullness of such an occupation, took it.

At first, of course, it was not easy for him. Nor did he all at once give up his old habits. But he persevered until he had so far got the better of them that he decided to go back to the hospital which had once turned him out. And this time there were no complaints. He stayed there for five years, helping to nurse the sick, and some one who saw him wrote, "I know not what more the

most loving mother could have done for her sick child."
He determined to go one step further and become a
priest, and so he, who had been so lazy and rebellious in
his schooldays, went back to school at the age of thirty-
two and sat quietly among small boys, who nicknamed
him "the Late Arrival," learning Latin grammar.

Camillus's ambition was now to serve the poor and the
outcasts whom no one else cared for. Because of his

They went on to battlefields

early life, he understood them and knew how terrible for
them sickness could be. So he gathered round him
others who thought as he did, and they made a vow that
wherever there was pain and illness and death, no matter
how dangerous the place, they would go to the rescue.
On their shoulders they wore the Red Cross of the Crusaders, and with this as their badge they went into vile
dens, where people were dying of the plague, into prisons,
where men were condemned to death, on to battlefields,
among convicts in the galleys. Camillus's Congregation

of Nursing Brothers—or, as they were sometimes called, the Brothers of a Happy Death—was the original Red Cross movement. To Camillus, the one-time soldier, we owe the first field ambulances and advanced dressing-stations and field hospitals. But Camillus, the one-time down-and-out gambler, tried equally to help those who were what he once had been.

He still gambled, though in a different way. He took risks about people's goodness that no one else would take. Once, when he gave clothes to some ragged beggars, they immediately sold them and then started to run away before Camillus should see what they had done. But Camillus brought them back, and without a word gave them some more clothes. When people told him that this was going too far and that such men were beyond help, he said, "What, my brothers, do you see nothing but the rags of these poor creatures? And do you see nothing beneath the rags but the poor creatures themselves?" And then he reminded them of Jesus's saying, "Inasmuch as you have done it unto one of the least of these my brethren, you have done it unto me."

To the end Camillus served the outcast and the dying wherever they might be, because, in so doing, he was serving Christ Himself. When he could hardly move for the pain in his foot and was so ill that everything he ate made him sick he still managed to visit the beds of the dying and give them what help and comfort he could. And when he himself came to die he lay with them in a common infirmary. After asking men to pray for him, "a great sinner, a gambler and a man of bad life," the Saint stretched out his arms in the form of a cross, murmured the words, "Most Precious Blood," and died "without a shudder or change of his countenance."

LV

ST VINCENT DE PAUL

(ST VINCENT'S DAY: JULY 19)

IN the year 1576, when Blessed Edmund Campion was still studying at Prague and St Teresa still founding new convents in Spain, a boy named Vincent was born to a farmer in Pouy, a village in the south-west of

He was captured by Turkish pirates

France. Like St Joan, Vincent, when he was small, looked after his father's sheep; but his parents were quite sure he would never be a farmer, and though they were very poor, they managed to save enough money to send him to school. He studied hard and at last was able to go to a university in Spain, where he passed all his examinations and became a priest.

As he was coming back to France by sea the ship he was in was captured by Turkish pirates, and taken to Tunis in Africa; and Vincent, who was twenty-five, found himself in the slave-market, being sold as a slave. He was bought by a fisherman, who sold him to an old alchemist, and finally he belonged to a Frenchman who lived in Africa and had turned Mohammedan. Vincent converted his last master back to Faith; and together they escaped and managed to get back to France, where after more travels including a visit to Rome, Vincent became the parish priest of a little place not far from Paris called Clichy. But he did not stay there long. An important French nobleman, Gondi, sent for him to become tutor to his children. The two men became lifelong friends.

Gondi was the General of the Galleys—that is to say he was responsible for seeing that the king's ships were properly manned. In those days the galleys were rowed by convicts chained to their oars and continually whipped like animals when they showed signs of being tired. When they were not at sea they were crowded into damp dungeons with chains on their legs and given for their food only water and black bread.

Vincent persuaded Gondi to appoint him Chaplain to the Galleys, and immediately he got this position he set to work to bring hope into the lives of these hopeless men. He had known what it was to be a slave and, because of that, he was perhaps the only person in the whole of France who could have helped them. One day, when he was with Gondi visiting the fleet, one of the galley-slaves —so the story says—fainted at the oar. Vincent quietly took his place. The convicts learned to love and trust him. He served them in any way he could, doing what was possible to lessen their sufferings; and at last, by asking for money from the wealthy people he met in Gondi's palace, he built a hospital for them. But there were others besides galley-convicts who were poor and outcast and miserable. In Paris alone, four out of every fifty people had absolutely nothing they could call their own and only managed to keep alive by begging scraps to eat. There were thousands of children, whom their parents did not want, in institutions where they were ill-treated or died of hunger—or, even worse, made lame or blind or in some way deformed so that they could be used as sideshows in fairs or hired out to people who made them beg on the roadside. Then there were the country labourers, kept working like cattle so that they seemed like "black animals." And above all—for Vincent never forgot these—there were the Christian slaves in Africa, at least forty thousand of them, including many French and English boys.

Vincent wanted to help them all and he set about it in a very sensible way. He knew that the rich people he met were not really as selfish as they seemed. They just had not thought about the way they were treating the poor. Many of them were not as happy as they seemed either. The Court life, which seemed so gay and splendid, was often very dull and always very empty. So Vincent went to them and pleaded the cause of the poor and the outcast and especially of the children and the slaves. No one in all France's history had thought of doing this before in the way that Vincent did it. He asked the rich and the well-born for money and—what was more difficult—service. He got both. He got enough money to build hospitals, ransom slaves, train priests who would go into the countryside.

At first these priests lived together in a monastery dedicated to St Lazarus—the poor man who sat at the rich man's gate in the parable that Jesus had told. They were called Lazarists, and the part of Paris where they lived is still commemorated in the name of the railway-station which now stands there—Saint-Lazare. Vincent sent his Lazarists not only over all France but abroad to Ireland, up to the Scottish Hebrides, to Egypt and Brazil and Madagascar and China.

But the most extraordinary thing he did was to persuade many wealthy and famous women to give up their lives in the fashionable world and to visit and help the sick and poor. He called them his Sisters of Charity, and so many people joined them that they grew into a great order—and the wide white hats that Vincent made their "uniform" are still worn by those who do the same work now, three hundred years later.

It is not surprising that when the King of France, Louis XIII, knew that he was dying he sent for Vincent, so that he might die in his arms.

"O, Monsieur Vincent," he said, "if I am restored to health I shall appoint no bishops unless they have spent three years with you." And after his death Vincent was always asked who he thought should be made a bishop, so that the whole church in France might show the charity of Christ which had been so forgotten.

Vincent was over eighty when he himself died. He had become so feeble that he could only raise himself from his bed by a cord nailed to a hook in the ceiling. But he never stopped organizing his charities and seeing that all the money that now came to him was used as best it could be. He knew that his followers would see that the work went on.

"Ready," he used to whisper, thinking that death had come for him. And when at last it did come one September morning at four o'clock—the time when he always got up to pray—he said just, "I believe," then, "I trust," and did not speak again.

LVI

ST ALPHONSUS LIGUORI

(ST ALPHONSUS'S DAY: AUGUST 2)

ALPHONSUS was the eldest son of a naval officer, and was born at his father's country house near Naples in 1696. He was never sent to school, but was educated by tutors at home, so that his father could be sure that he worked properly at his lessons. As well as his lessons, he practised the harpsichord—the piano of those days—for three hours a day, and by the time he was thirteen could play like a master. All his life he had a great love for music, and later on he wrote and composed many hymns.

His father had determined that he should become a lawyer, and, as Alphonsus had a keen brain and was a good speaker, he enjoyed working hard for that too. He worked so hard, in fact, that he became a Doctor of Laws when he was only sixteen, though, as a rule, no one was allowed to do this before they were twenty. He was at the time so small that he could hardly be seen in his doctor's robes, and all the people laughed at him. But they did not laugh long. By the time he was just over twenty he was one of the leading lawyers in Naples.

In the year 1723 there was a great law-suit between the Grand Duke of Tuscany and a nobleman of Naples about some property worth a hundred thousand pounds. Alphonsus, who, they said, had never lost a case, was the leading lawyer on one side, and after he had made a brilliant opening speech he sat down, quite sure he had won again, and waiting for the witnesses to be called. But his opponent did not call any witnesses. He just said,

"Your arguments are a waste of breath. You have overlooked a document which destroys your whole case."

"What document is that?" said Alphonsus. "Let me see it."

His opponent handed him the paper, and when Alphonsus read it he turned pale. It was nothing new. It was something he had read over and over again, but he saw now that he had thought it meant exactly the opposite of what it did mean.

He became a Doctor of Laws when he was only sixteen

"You are right," he said. "I made a mistake. This document gives you the case."

He left the law-court almost in tears. He thought his career would be ruined. People would imagine not that he, the most brilliant of the lawyers of Naples, had made a careless mistake, but that he had really been deceitful and bribed by the other side. He swore that he would never appear as a lawyer again, and for three days he would neither eat anything nor see anyone.

Then he realized that perhaps this humiliation had been sent by God to break his pride, and that God wanted him to serve Him in some special way. He prayed a great deal that he might know God's will, and one day when he was visiting the sick in the Hospital for Incurables—which he did every week—he was given the answer. He found himself surrounded by a mysterious light; the house seemed to shake, and he heard a voice in his heart saying, "Leave the world, and give yourself to Me." This happened twice, and when he had finished his visit he went straight to a church, laid his sword before a statue of Our Lady, and promised to become a priest.

He was only twenty-six at the time. He was ordained priest at the age of thirty, and he lived until he was ninety-one the kind of life he promised to lead—one in which he would never waste a single minute.

His first work was to teach the peasants in the country districts round about, and this led to the founding of a new Order in the Church—the Congregation of the Most Holy Redeemer, who are generally known as the Redemptorists. Then, when he was fifty-six, the Pope insisted on making him Bishop of a diocese lying just off the road between Naples and Capua, known as St Agatha of the Goths, which, in spite of illness after illness which in the end left him paralysed, he ruled till he was nearly eighty. And, in spite of all the work he had to do among people who did not really know about the Faith or want to lead good lives, he managed to write book after book, and use all the learning he had and his sharp, trained lawyer's mind and his love of music for the glory of God.

LVII

ST BENEDICT JOSEPH LABRE

(ST BENEDICT'S DAY: APRIL 16)

BENEDICT JOSEPH was the eldest son of a prosperous farmer. He was born in 1748 in the village of Amettes, in the north of France. From the beginning he was a rather odd little boy. He played games and learnt lessons like every one else, and all his life he was of a happy nature; but he seemed to like giving things away more than getting them and to see how much he could do without. In the coldest weather, his mother noticed, he would deliberately sit as far away from the fire as he could. He liked talking to tramps and beggars. Even in his lessons he was only really interested in those about Jesus and the saints and the Church.

When he was twelve he went to live with his uncle, who was the parish priest of Erin not far away from his home, and who thought that Benedict might himself one day become a priest. For six years he stayed there, learning Latin, studying the Scriptures, helping his uncle in the church, until, when he was eighteen, there was an epidemic in the town. His uncle went about among the sick and dying, taking the Blessed Sacrament to them; and at first he allowed Benedict to go with him. Then he became afraid that the boy might catch the infection, so he would not let him come any more into the homes of the dying. But Benedict felt he must do something to help, and spent his time looking after all the cattle of sick villagers, driving the flocks to pasture, cleaning out the cowsheds, and seeing to their fodder. When his uncle caught the plague and died Benedict went home to his parents and his fourteen brothers and sisters.

But Benedict had no intention of staying at home. He had made up his mind that he wanted to give himself to God in the most difficult way he could think of—in the absolute poverty, silence, and fasting of the monastery of La Trappe, where the Rule was the strictest in the world. His father and mother, though they were disappointed that he was not going to be a parish priest and stay near the family, at last said he might go if he wanted; and so he set out to become a Trappist. But when he arrived at the monastery they would not have him. They thought he was too young and looked too delicate to be able to stand the hardship of the life, and told him to go home.

His parents were delighted to see him, and for a little while Benedict went on with his studies under the charge of another uncle. But he became more and more sure that he was not meant to be a parish priest. He went away again to another monastery where the Rule was not so strict; but again they sent him home. This happened again and again, and at last Benedict realized that he was not meant to be a monk either.

But what did God want him to be? Benedict decided that he would be God's tramp. He would behave in the world as though he were in a monastery. He would keep silent; he would own nothing; he would go along the roads of Europe, thinking of God and visiting all the shrines where he could to make special prayers for all the unhappy people of the world.

So, twenty-five years old, he set out, clad in an old cloak tied round his waist with a rope, with a large rosary round his neck and a small one in his hand, and on his back a sack which had in it a breviary, a Bible, and his favourite book, *The Imitation of Christ*. He took nothing else. He never begged, though he took any food that was given him, giving away to other tramps any that he did not need. He slept always in the open in the summer, though in the winter he would accept a bed if anyone offered it to him. But, as in course of time his clothes became dirty and more and more ragged and he did not look or smell very clean, fewer and fewer people wanted anything to do with him.

He travelled on the road like a beggar

In this way he tramped over France, through Switzerland, and into Italy. He visited Germany and Spain and, year by year, he made his way to Rome.

It was in Rome in the year 1782 that a priest named Marconi met him. He wrote a description of him. Benedict at first sight, he says, looked "decidedly unpleasant and forbidding. His legs were only partially covered, his clothes were tied round his waist with an old cord. His hair was uncombed, he was ill-clad and wrapped about in an old and ragged coat. In his outward appearance he seemed to be the most miserable beggar I had ever seen."

But Father Marconi became Benedict's confessor, and he very soon realized that this was no ordinary tramp like the hundreds that swarmed about the churches of Rome, though he did not know, any more than anyone else knew, how near to God Benedict had grown in his strange wanderings.

On the Wednesday in Holy Week in the next year, 1783, Benedict was at Mass as usual, but he was so weak that he was hardly able to stand through the long passage from the Gospels telling of Jesus's trial and death, which is read on that day. The people round him were expecting this starved-looking tramp to collapse, but somehow Benedict managed to remain on his feet. Only as he left the church did he fall on the steps and find he was too weak to get up. They carried him into the house of a butcher who lived nearby, and in a few hours he was dead.

Then a most extraordinary thing happened. Almost immediately the children in the street where he had died started calling out: "The Saint is dead! The Saint is dead!" And all the city took up the cry. Nothing like it had ever been seen in Rome. That Wednesday evening, as soon as Benedict's body had been carried into the same church where in the morning he had stood through the reading from the Gospels, the crowds were so great that a special detachment of police had to be hurried there to control them. For four days these crowds grew. Cardinals, noblemen, visitors from other lands—from the whole world, it seemed—came to stand by the coffin of Benedict, the Tramp of God. Within twelve weeks of his death he had performed 136 miraculous cures which no one was able to deny. (It is one of the signs of saints that they perform miracles after their deaths; and no one is ever proclaimed a saint unless such miracles are absolutely proved.) And in less than a year the newspapers of London and of all the capitals of Europe were

discussing the story of the young Frenchman whom in
life no one had noticed, and who had deliberately become the loneliest and poorest of the tramps on the roads
so that nothing in the world could come between him
and God.

LVIII

THE CURÉ D'ARS

(St John Baptist Vianney)

WHEN St Benedict Joseph Labre first set out on his pilgrimages he was given a bowl of soup and shelter for the night by a farmer in one of the villages he passed through. The farmer's name was Vianney, and the village was Dardilly, not far from Lyons. Sixteen years later—three years after St Benedict's death—the farmer's grandson was born in that same house and baptized John Baptist; and when he grew up one of his treasures was the letter of thanks which St Benedict had written to his grandfather. But young Vianney had no idea that he too was to become a saint—though a saint of a very different kind. St Benedict Joseph Labre was a wanderer over Europe; St John Baptist Vianney was to stay all his life as a priest in one tiny French village, Ars; and that is why he is known in history as the Curé d'Ars—the Vicar of Ars.

When he was three the French Revolution broke out. The people of Paris turned against the Church. They destroyed the shrine of St Denis, the patron of France; they broke open the tomb of St Geneviève, burnt her body, and turned her church into a pagan Hall of Fame, which they called the Panthéon; they made it a crime to hold any Church services, and executed any priests who were caught saying Mass. So to little John Baptist Vianney being a priest meant just what it had meant to St Denis and his companions fifteen hundred years before—being some one who risked his life to do what Jesus had told him to do. There in Dardilly they were sometimes able to hear Mass secretly in a barn when a priest could visit them; but John was ten years old before he was able to make his first Communion. But of one thing he was quite certain: the only thing he wanted was to be a priest.

He was not a clever boy. He found lessons very difficult, and though, when the Revolution was over and Napoleon allowed the churches to open again, he studied hard at his lessons, he did not think he would ever pass his examinations. Then there came another blow to his hopes. Students for the priesthood were not conscripted for the Army; but as, just at that time, Napoleon wanted every soldier he could get for his war in Spain, this rule was broken. John must go to the wars like all the other young men.

On the morning his regiment left he went into the church as usual to say his prayers, and by the time he came out the rest had gone. In trying to catch them up, he took the wrong road and found himself, not with the Army, but in a town where a lot of deserters had hidden themselves. There he had to stay until news of it got back to his home, and his younger brother offered to go to the war in his place so that John could go back to his studies for the priesthood.

At last with great difficulty he managed to pass his examinations, and was made a priest about two months after the battle of Waterloo.

Because he was not very clever the Bishop sent him in 1818 to the little town of Ars, and there John Baptist Vianney settled down to be the parish priest. He was glad that it was a small, out-of-the-way place with simple people, where no one would notice him or expect much of him. But one thing he determined: he really would be the parish priest and look after every soul in his parish.

He loved them all, and because he loved them he was
not afraid to be angry with them when they had done
wrong. Gradually he made them such good Christians
that the people who lost money when the villagers
stopped getting drunk and riotous and worldly tried to
drive him away. But he stayed there—and suddenly Ars,
of which no one outside the district had heard, became

He prayed in church before the regiment left

talked about. People started coming from other places
in France to see this remarkable Curé and to ask his
advice.

They went home and told their friends that in Ars
there was a priest who could see into people's souls.
Soon it was not only from France they came, but from
all Europe—twenty thousand visitors a year—coming to
try to make their confessions to the Curé d'Ars. He had
to sit in his confessional for between sixteen and eighteen

hours a day; he seldom had time for more than two hours' sleep; he ate so little that he looked almost transparent—but for forty-one years he stayed—until he died there, never thinking of himself, trying to help people to find God.

LIX

ST BERNADETTE

(ST BERNADETTE'S DAY: APRIL 16)

BERNADETTE SOUBIROUS was the daughter of a miller in the town of Lourdes. When she was born the family was quite prosperous, but the father was a ne'er-do-well, and by the time that Bernadette was thirteen they were living in a slum—a single, stone-walled room about five yards square with two small windows opening on a courtyard where there was a manure heap. "They were poorer than I can say," wrote a cousin, "—two poor beds, one on the right hand near the door, the other on the same side near the chimney; a little old box containing their linen; a few terracotta plates; and that was about all."

What was worse, the father was put in prison for a short time, and the townsmen considered the Soubirous family very unpleasant people. It did not matter that they were poor; they were the wrong kind of poor— down-and-outs, who were hardly worth helping. However hard the mother tried, the slum room could not be kept free from vermin. However good the children tried to be, they were always hungry—one of Bernadette's brothers was found eating the votive candles in the church—and no one thought of them as anything but "bad stock."

One day, when she was fourteen, Bernadette went out with her sister and another girl to gather some firewood from a little copse; but a woman there told them not to trespass. There was plenty of wood, she said, washed up by the river near a rock with a little grotto in it. The children ran off to find it and, as the river was a mere trickle at one point, they took off their shoes and paddled across. But Bernadette, who had a bad cough and had been told by her mother not to get wet, did not go with them. She asked her friend, who was bigger than she was, to carry her across; but the girl would not and shouted: "You can cross as we did." In spite of her cold, Bernadette did not want to be left behind; so she took her stockings off and was just going to cross when she heard a noise like a great gust of wind and saw the bush on the rock above the grotto waving about. Behind it was something white, and Bernadette, looking closely, realized that it was a Lady.

"She had a white veil which came to her feet," said Bernadette later, when she was describing it. "I saw a yellow rose on each foot. She kept her hands slightly apart and held a rosary. She was young. Her face and clothes reminded me of a statue of Our Lady before which I used to pray, but she was alive and had light all round her. I gazed hard for a moment, then knelt down, and started praying. She smiled at me and withdrew into the biggest opening above the grotto."

When the others came back with their firewood she asked them if they had seen anything. But they had not, and Bernadette whispered to her sister what had happened. That evening, when Bernadette was saying her prayers at home, she suddenly burst out crying and was so upset that her sister told her mother what had happened during the afternoon. All her mother said was that she must have been dreaming, and the family told Bernadette not to be a silly little girl but to forget all about it.

But Bernadette could not forget. She was quite sure she had not been dreaming. She went back to the grotto, and again she saw the Lady. Other people went with her and, though they saw nothing, they realized that Bernadette was seeing and talking to some one.

Some of the people thought Bernadette was ill, some that she was a little mad; more thought it was only a trick that the unpleasant Soubirous family were trying to play on the rest of Lourdes so that they could get talked about and perhaps get some money. But however they tried to prevent it, Bernadette kept going back to the place and praying and hoping to see the Lady.

The vision appeared

It was on February 11, 1858, that the first vision appeared. By March 4, Bernadette had seen the Lady sixteen times, and there was a crowd of twenty thousand people watching her pray there. That great crowd had come to believe her because of something that had happened on February 25. On that day, the people had seen Bernadette crawl on her knees up and down the cave, then start down to the river, then turn back again to the cave, and scrape the mud at the bottom of a dirty puddle, from which she drank and daubed her face.

After this the people of Lourdes were quite sure the little girl was mad. For they had not seen the Lady or heard her say to Bernadette: "Go and drink at the fountain, and wash yourself in it."

When Bernadette had started to go to the river to wash and drink the Lady said that that was not the spring she meant, and she pointed to a spot in the cave. All that Bernadette could see there was a dirty puddle, but she knew that she must do as the Lady told her. When the crowds asked her why she had done it she simply said: "I have no idea. The Lady told me to."

Most of the people went away in disgust; but a few stayed behind, sorry for Bernadette and wondering what would happen next. They were the few who saw the muddy puddle turn into a little stream of clear water, which bubbled up from a spring which no one had known of till the Lady pointed it out to Bernadette.

A few hours later an old stone-mason of Lourdes, hearing of the finding of this new spring, sent his daughter to bring him some of the water. He had lost the sight of one eye twenty years before. When he bathed his eye in the spring-water it was healed at once. All Lourdes soon knew of the miracle, which was the first of thousands; and to-day from all over the world the sick come to be cured and to pray at Our Lady's Grotto where the water flows which was discovered because of the obedience of a little slum-girl of fourteen—St Bernadette.

LX

ST JOHN BOSCO

(ST JOHN BOSCO'S DAY: JANUARY 31)

IT was in the year of the battle of Waterloo, 1815, that John Bosco was born in a little cabin in a hillside village not far from Turin. His father died when he was two, and his mother, who was very poor, had two other children to bring up; so John's first years were spent as a shepherd boy. Although he had very little time to study, he knew when he was quite young that he wanted to become a priest. He was only nine when he had a strange dream in which he saw himself changing a crowd of children from beasts into lambs and heard a voice saying, "Not with blows, but with gentleness." He took this to mean that he was in some way to give his life to looking after rough children.

He was so certain that he started at once to find ways to get other boys' attention and interest. He learnt to walk the tight-rope and to become an acrobat; he made himself a first-class conjuror and an athlete who could beat professionals; and when the time came that he could attract crowds he would follow the entertainment by saying the rosary or giving a simple little sermon.

In his spare time he studied as hard as he could, and, though he had no money to pay for a proper education, it was at last provided for him, and he became a priest when he was twenty-six.

While he had been training for the priesthood in Turin he had seen in the slums there the wretchedness and poverty and crime and evil among which thousands of boys had to live, and he longed more than ever to be able to help them. But they would have nothing to do with the Church or with priests, and there was no way by which he could get to them. Then one day just after he had been made priest he was getting ready to say Mass, and the sacristan was talking to a ragged boy who had come into the church, asking him to serve at the altar. The boy, who was rather stupid, said he did not know how to, and the sacristan lost his temper, boxed his ears, and told him to go home.

Bosco turned on the sacristan and said sharply, "I won't have my friends treated like that!"

"Your *friend*, Father? I'm sorry. I didn't know he was a friend of yours."

"The moment anyone is ill-treated he becomes my friend," said Bosco, and sent the sacristan running after the boy to call him back.

Next Sunday the boy, whose name was Bartholomew, came to the church, bringing some of his friends with him. More and more came, the roughest boys of the Turin streets, to see this young priest who was the first person they had known to treat them kindly. Bosco played games with them, taught them, helped them, and in three years his 'school' was numbered in hundreds.

This was the beginning of Bosco's work among poor children which soon spread throughout the whole world; for by the time he died in 1888 over 120,000 children were being cared for and trained in various countries by the Order of St Francis de Sales—the Salesians—which the Saint founded in order to look after them. But the first years were not so easy, because then no one wanted John Bosco and his horde of ragged ruffians anywhere near them. People complained, and time after time they had to move. They were even turned out of a chapel they had been given near some mills, because the millers complained that they did not want people of that kind anywhere near them. The authorities even tried to shut Bosco up in an asylum. On one occasion an attempt was made to murder him as he sat teaching; but the bullet missed and only ripped the edge of his cassock.

"A pity," he said. "It was my best cassock."

He made himself a first-class conjuror

But through all dangers he was preserved, though sometimes it seemed only by a miracle. And one of his strangest guardians was a large, wild, mongrel dog called Grigio which insisted on going with him through dangerous places. On one occasion Grigio turned on him, snarling, and refused to allow him to leave the room. Afterwards it was discovered that if he had gone

229

out at that time, as he intended, he would have been ambushed and killed.

One of Bosco's last thoughts was for England, and the year before his death the first Salesian House was founded in this country, at Roehampton.

LXI

ST THÉRÈSE OF LISIEUX

(ST THÉRÈSE'S DAY: OCTOBER 3)

NOTHING could have been more different from the poor home of Bernadette Soubirous than the large, comfortable house of Thérèse Martin. M. Martin was a wealthy watchmaker, who, when his wife died, leaving him with five girls (of whom Thérèse was the youngest), retired to the town of Lisieux; and there in a big house standing in a great garden with lawns and flowers and trees he settled down to bring up his children.

Thérèse and her sisters, Marie, Pauline, Léonie, and Céline, were able to have most of the things they wanted; but their father brought them up to understand that what they should want most of all was to please God; and when Pauline was twenty-one she decided to become a nun in the Carmelite convent at Lisieux. When ten-year-old Thérèse heard this she started to cry very bitterly. Pauline was her "little mother," who had brought her up after their mother died; Pauline was her favourite sister; but above all, ever since she could remember she and Pauline had played at being hermits and had always said they would go away together. And now Pauline was going alone and leaving her.

But she had to wait only five years before she joined Pauline again, and herself became a nun in the Carmelite convent of the town. That was a very early age for anyone to enter; but her father was willing that she should go, and when she and her father and her sister Céline were on a visit to Rome she actually asked the Pope.

"Holy Father," she asked, as she knelt before him in

audience, "I have a great favour to ask. In honour of your Jubilee, allow me to become a Carmelite when I am fifteen."

"My child," said the Pope, "you must do as the Superiors decide."

"Holy Father," persisted Thérèse, "if only you will say yes every one else will agree."

"If it be God's will," said the Pope, "you shall enter."

She wrote the story of her life

And three months after her fifteenth birthday she entered.

Ten years later she died, and if it had not been that her sister Pauline, who was Prioress for some of the time, had ordered her to write her autobiography we should know nothing about her life. But because of this book we know how she tried to live and all about her "Little Way," as it is called. This meant that she tried to please God in the very smallest things of her life, because she understood that everything that happened to her was His will and His gift. If she were scolded or blamed she would not answer back. If she had any sorrow or disappointment she would not show it. She changed a pretty jug in her cell for an ugly, cracked one, because another Sister liked hers. However ill or tired she felt, she would never complain.

When she was dying she said: "I feel that my mission is soon to begin—to teach my Little Way to souls. I want to spend my heaven in doing good on earth. There can be no rest for me till the end of the world."

Almost as soon as she was dead many miracles happened, and the world knew that the girl who had always tried "never to refuse God anything" was a saint.

LXII

ST PIUS THE TENTH

(ST PIUS'S DAY: AUGUST 20)

ST PIUS X, the Pope who died just after the outbreak of the Great War of 1914–18, was born at Riese in 1835. His name was Giuseppe Sarto, and he was the son of the village postman. Later when he became Pope and was leading so good a life that people called him "Saint" in his lifetime he used to remind them in a joking form of his real name. When he heard them refer to him as "Papa santo" (the holy Pope) he would say, "You have got one letter wrong; I am Papa Sarto."

Even as a very little boy he had that kind of quick wit. Once, during catechism the parish priest had said, "I will give an apple to anyone who can tell me where God is." Before anyone could answer Giuseppe jumped up and said, "And I will give two apples to anyone who can tell me where God is not."

From his childhood, too, he wanted to be a priest. He never missed serving Mass, and when he was a schoolboy he would get up very early to attend it in his parish church; then he would go home to breakfast before he set off for his four-mile walk to school, which he often made barefoot to make the leather on his sandals last longer—for he was very poor.

When he became Pope one of the first things he did was to make it possible for boys and girls to receive Holy Communion as soon as they could understand what it meant. There had grown up a wrong custom of not allowing them to do so until they were about twelve. Even when he was just a parish priest Giuseppe Sarto had not followed this custom, but had followed St

234

Thomas Aquinas, who had written in his great book, "As soon as a child knows the difference between the Bread of Christ and ordinary bread he may receive Holy Communion." As Pope Pius X he reminded the whole world of this by a special decree, and he told some friends that the happiest moment of his life was something that happened because of it.

The Pope, with tears in his eyes, said good-bye to students

Four hundred French children, none of whom was much more than seven years old, made a special pilgrimage to Rome to thank him for it, bringing with them an album which 135,000 other children had signed. A special service was held for them in Rome, during which the preacher said, "Emperors and kings have come to Rome in order to kneel before the Vicar of Christ; knights and crusaders have come to beg his blessing; representatives of all nations have come to pay their respects to the Head of the Church; but never till this day has a crusade of children come to the Holy City to thank His Holiness for a benefit he has given them."

Most of Giuseppe Sarto's life was spent in teaching and in trying to get other people to teach the Christian faith. He saw that people were forgetting it and taking so much interest in other kinds of learning that they would bring evil times on the world. When they said to him that perhaps he was not interested enough in the clever things people were doing and saying he answered, "I am only a poor peasant and have only one point of view—the Crucifix."

When the evil times came and the Great War broke out the Pope, with tears in his eyes, said good-bye to students in Rome who were returning to their own countries to fight. He blessed English, French, Germans, Austrians, Slavs, Belgians, all standing before him, united in love for him, but knowing that in a few months they would be fighting against each other. "Show yourselves worthy of the faith you profess," he said, "and in war do not forget mercy."

A fortnight later he was dead, broken-hearted.

LXIII

ST FRANCES XAVIER

(MOTHER CABRINI)

FRANCES CABRINI was a farmer's daughter who was born near Lodi, in Lombardy, in 1850. She was the youngest child of the family, and from very early days she wanted to become a missionary. Once, when she was a little girl picnicking by the river, she decided to turn the waxed paper in which the food had been wrapped into paper-boats. It was, of course, something that any child might have done. But Frances filled each boat with masses of wild violets, and when her elder sister said she was being silly and that they would all sink and scatter on the water, she answered: "God will take care of them. They're missionaries. They'll go all the way to China." Even then she was thinking of the great missionary work of St Francis Xavier, and wanting to follow in his footsteps. And always it was to the Far East that she dreamed of going. When she went to school the only subject she was really good at and interested in was geography. Later, when she offered herself to the Bishop, hoping he would allow her to fulfil her ambition, he sent her first to take charge of an orphanage near her home; and when at last, as a woman of thirty-nine, she gained permission to go abroad, it was not to the East she was sent, but to the West—to the United States of America. Already she had founded the Order of Missionary Sisters of the Sacred Heart, and it was in connexion with this that she first visited the Pope, Leo XIII. It was he who told her: "Not East but West," and in obedience to him she, with some of her nuns, set sail for America to work among the Italians who had emigrated there, and who were working in such bad conditions that they were almost like slaves and had lost their faith in their religion.

She arrived in New York on March 31, 1889, after an unpleasant voyage, only to find that there was no convent ready for her. There had been some misunderstanding, and the Archbishop of New York suggested that she should return to Italy. But when she showed

She insisted on helping to pack them up

him the Pope's order to her he changed his mind, and found a home for her with some Sisters of Charity.

Mother Cabrini, however, was determined to have her own convent from which to look after orphans and minister to the inhabitants of "Little Italy," as the Italian quarter of New York was called, and she managed, in the end, to take over a house which the Jesuits no longer needed. Her Order was established in America, at last, and she herself became an American citizen. But this was not the end of her missionary journeys. She returned more than once to Europe; she crossed the Andes on a mule-train; she sailed to South America. In 1898 she visited London, and fell in love with England and the English: "In other countries they speak of nobility and courtesy," she said; "in England they practise it. God will bless this nation and give it the grace of re-entering the One True Church." In 1902 the first English convent of her Order was opened in Southwark.

Mother Cabrini died in Chicago on December 21, 1917, during the First World War. Just before her death she had been told that more than five hundred children of Italian immigrants would have no Christmas gifts. She gave an order that presents were to be bought for them out of the funds of the Convent, and though very ill, she insisted on helping to pack them up. She was able to complete this before, that winter morning, she collapsed into her chair and died.

She was canonized under the name of St Frances Xavier, in 1946—the first citizen of the United States to be pronounced a saint—and at the ceremony were several Chinese who had joined her order. She had, in God's way, missionized in China in the steps of St Francis Xavier, as she had wished.